JERKIN'
IT

HARRY COX

JERKIN' IT

A (FORKIN' FUNNY)
MOUTHWATERING
BBQ COOKBOOK
THAT WILL LEAVE
MEAT LOVERS
STUFFED AND
SATISFIED

ULYSSES PRESS

LONG-HANDLED TONGS. If you can't find the Magnum grill tongs, the regular long-handled version will work just fine. Look for sturdy, spring-loaded tongs that can hold up to turning even the heaviest of meats.

MEAT THERMOMETER. The best way to tell when your meat is cooked to perfection is with a meat thermometer. Gently slide it into the thickest, moistest part of your meat for the most accurate temperature.

GRILL HOE. Your grill hoe is essential for moving around scorching coals without burning yourself. She may be a hoe, but you'll need her for when things get really hot and heavy.

GRILLING GLOVES. A pair of heavy suede grilling gloves will protect your more delicate appendages from getting burned by passionate heat.

CHARCOAL. "Briquettes" are best, since they burn more evenly and can go All. Night. Long.

WOOD CHIPS. These are best for a smoker and will keep your meat nice and flavorful.

HOT TIPS FOR HANDLING YOUR MEAT

- Remember to tease your meat up to room temperature for a good 30 minutes before grilling.
- Light charcoal grills 1 hour before the magic happens, so the coals have time to produce a nice and even heat.
- Turn foods and cook 'em real good for the same amount of time on each side.
- Give your meat a rest before you dive in, allowing all the juices to stay put.
- And when in doubt, wrap it up—with some aluminum foil—especially when dealing with delicate vegetables and fish.

RUB IT OUT! OR KEEP IT SPICY?

Below you'll find a list of the top ten naughtiest spices we've EVER had—and the ones you'll most likely need before you fire up the grill:

- salt
- pepper
- paprika
- garlic powder
- onion powder

- chili powder
- crushed red pepper
- cumin
- cinnamon
- various dried herbs (sage, rosemary, oregano, basil, cilantro, etc.)

This is my go-to recipe to impress a date when we decide to stay in and cook together. I don't always cook for my dates, but when I do I turn to my trusty, no-fail, and guaranteed-to-get-you-laid tri-tip steak. When grilled to juicy, medium perfection, the dish will serve as a teaser to the main entrée of your evening.

PRO TIP: Serve with a lighter side, like a salad or grilled vegetables, so you don't end up being your own cock block.

GRILL: ANY GRILL | PREP TIME: 5 MINUTES | CHILL TIME: OVERNIGHT | COOK TIME: 8 TO 12 MINUTES | MAKES: 4 STEAKS

1½ to 2½ pounds triangle roast

⅓ cup lemon juice

2 tablespoons olive oil

2 tablespoons Worcestershire sauce

2 tablespoons honey

2 teaspoons onion powder

2 teaspoons Italian seasoning

1 teaspoon salt

1 teaspoon ground black pepper

8 cloves garlic, minced

1 large handful of fresh cilantro leaves

3 green onions or additional fresh cilantro, for garnish (optional)

INSTRUCTIONS

1. Rinse the roast and pat it dry with a paper towel, then place it in a one-gallon ziplock bag.

2. Add the four liquid ingredients to the bag, followed by the four dried seasonings, and finally the garlic and cilantro leaves.

3. Seal the bag and passionately shake it until the meat is smothered in juices. Reopen the bag to release the air, then, reseal the bag and let the meat rest and cool down in the refrigerator overnight.

4. Preheat the grill to high. If using a charcoal grill, let the charcoal burn for about 10 minutes, until covered with white-gray ash to reach high heat.

5. Pat the roast lightly with a paper towel and place it on the open flames. Cook for 5 to 10 minutes on each side.

6. Remove the roast from the heat and let rest for 2 to 3 minutes.

7. Where the grain meets, slice the tri-tips against the grain.

8. Garnish with green onions or additional fresh cilantro.

9. Serve immediately and watch your date enjoy their first taste of your meat.

This seared meat takes things to the next level. It will be the juiciest piece of meat you've ever had in your mouth. All it takes is a little preparation to submerge the bone-in beef in the tasty, savory sauce and let those juices absorb all night long.

GRILL: ANY GRILL | PREP TIME: 10 MINUTES | CHILL TIME: OVERNIGHT | COOK TIME: 6 TO 10 MINUTES | MAKES: 4 SERVINGS

4 porterhouse steaks

6 tablespoons olive oil

6 tablespoons balsamic vinegar

1 tablespoon Worcestershire sauce

1 cup orange juice, no pulp

1 teaspoon salt

1 teaspoon ground black pepper

2 teaspoons garlic powder

1 teaspoon onion powder

1 teaspoon dried thyme

1 teaspoon dried rosemary

2 teaspoons Italian seasoning

fresh Italian parsley, for garnish

HORSERADISH SAUCE

½ cup sour cream

2 tablespoons mayonnaise

1 teaspoon white wine vinegar

2 tablespoons prepared horseradish, drained

¼ teaspoon salt

¼ teaspoon ground black pepper

1 tablespoon dried parsley

INSTRUCTIONS

1. Prepare the horseradish sauce by combining all the ingredients and stirring until completely incorporated. Set aside to chill overnight.

2. For the steak: rinse the steak and pat dry with a paper towel. No wet meat here.

3. Place the steak in a ziplock bag.

4. Pour in the four liquid ingredients, in order. Seal the bag and shake it vigorously.

5. Open the bag and add the seven seasoning ingredients.

6. Reseal the bag, shake it well, and tenderly massage the marinade into the meat.

7. Make sure the air is pressed from the bag. Let the meat absorb those tasty juices. Chill overnight.

8. Preheat the grill to high.

9. Lightly oil the grate with olive oil.

10. Place the steaks on the open flames portion of the grill and cook for 3 to 5 minutes, searing the meat.

11. Flip the meat and cook for another 3 to 5 minutes or until the internal temperature reaches 150°F.

12. Remove from the grill, plate, and serve with the horseradish sauce.

13. Garnish with parsley, if desired.

This gyro is a real hero. Just because the gyro meat is long and thin doesn't mean it will be lacking in the flavor department. The real superstar of this stuffed sandwich is the tangy, creamy white sauce, *tzatziki*. I'm talking about the homemade tzatziki!

GRILL: GAS | PREP TIME: 25 MINUTES | CHILL TIME: 2 HOURS + 2 HOURS | COOK TIME: 1 HOUR + 8 TO 10 MINUTES | MAKES: 10 SERVINGS

GYRO MEAT

½ white onion, cut into chunks

1 pound ground beef

1 pound ground lamb

2 tablespoons minced garlic

2 teaspoons dried oregano

2 teaspoons ground cumin

1 teaspoon dried marjoram

1½ teaspoons dried rosemary

1 teaspoon dried thyme

1½ teaspoons ground black pepper

½ teaspoon salt

TZATZIKI SAUCE

16 ounces plain Greek yogurt

1 medium cucumber, peeled, seeded, and finely chopped

4 cloves garlic, minced

⅛ teaspoon salt

2 tablespoons olive oil

2 teaspoons white wine vinegar

5 mint leaves, finely minced

GYROS

10 pitas

2 cups romaine lettuce, thinly chopped

2 tomatoes, thinly sliced

1 red onion, thinly sliced

½ cup cilantro leaves

sour cream (optional)

½ cup green or black olives (optional)

TO MAKE THE TZATZIKI SAUCE

1. Put the yogurt into a dish towel. Gather up the edges, suspend the towel over a bowl, wrapping it around the edge using rubber bands or twine to keep it in place, and refrigerate for 2 hours while the yogurt drains.

2. Put the chopped cucumber into another dish towel. Squeeze out the liquid and discard it like a used condom.

3. Put the drained yogurt and cucumber into a medium mixing bowl. Add the remaining ingredients and combine thoroughly.

4. Set aside in the refrigerator.

TO MAKE THE GYROS

1. Put the chunks of onion into a food processor. Process until finely chopped.

2. Scoop the onions out into a dish towel. Gather up the ends and squeeze the liquid out of the onions.

3. Dump the onions into a medium mixing bowl. Add the lamb and beef.

4. Add the seasonings to the bowl and get handsy, mixing it all together until fully incorporated.

5. Cover the meat and refrigerate for 2 hours to allow the flavors to blend.

6. Preheat the oven to 325°F.

7. Put the meat mixture into the food processor and pulse for 1 minute until finely chopped. The mixture should feel tacky.

8. Form the meat into a loaf shape and put on top of 2 overlapping pieces of plastic wrap that are 18 inches long.

9. Roll the mixture in the wrap rightly. Make sure there are no air pockets in the meat.

10. Pack the meat tightly into a 7x4-inch loaf pan. Be sure there are no air pockets in the pan. Twist the ends of the plastic wrap until the surface of the wrap is tight.

11. Refrigerate overnight to firm it up thoroughly.

12. Preheat the oven to high.

13. Put the meat on a rotisserie skewer. Put a double-thick piece of aluminum foil, folded into a tray, directly under the meat to catch drippings.

14. Cook on high for 15 minutes.

15. Reduce the heat to medium. Cook the meat for another 30 minutes or until the internal temperature reaches 165°F.

16. Turn the heat off and let the meat spin for another 15 minutes, or until the internal temperature hits 175°F.

17. Let it cool for 10 minutes, then slice thinly.

18. While the meat is cooling, plate your pitas. Smear creamy tzatziki sauce on the pitas, then layer lettuce, tomatoes, onions, and cilantro on the pita.

19. Add the thinly sliced meat to the pitas and dollop with sour cream, if desired.

20. Garnish with olives, as desired, and serve.

Girth over length any day. Need I say more?

GRILL: CHARCOAL GRILL OR SMOKER | PREP TIME: 15 MINUTES | COOK TIME: 23 MINUTES + 2 HOURS, 45 MINUTES | MAKES: 4 SERVINGS

BBQ SAUCE

1 (15-ounce) can tomato sauce

1 (6-ounce) can tomato paste

²/₃ cup light brown sugar, packed

¼ cup apple cider vinegar

1 tablespoon Worcestershire sauce

¼ teaspoon ground black pepper

1 teaspoon paprika

2 teaspoons garlic powder

1 teaspoon onion powder

½ cayenne pepper

½ teaspoon salt

RIBS

2 handfuls of cherry wood chips for smoky flavor

4 beef ribs

½ cup brown sugar, packed

4 tablespoons garlic powder

2 teaspoons cayenne pepper

4 teaspoons paprika

2 tablespoons onion powder

2 teaspoons ground black pepper

2 teaspoons ground mustard

3 tablespoons chili powder

4 teaspoons salt

TO MAKE THE BBQ SAUCE

1. Combine all the ingredients in a medium saucepan.

2. Bring the heat to medium-high.

3. Stir consistently for 2 minutes, then let the sauce rest until it begins to boil, about 4 minutes.

4. When boiling, turn down the heat to low and let it simmer for 15 minutes.

5. Remove it from the heat and let it cool for 5 minutes before using to baste the ribs.

TO MAKE THE RIBS

1. As you load in your charcoal, add 2 handfuls of cherry wood chips to add some delicious smoky flavor.

2. Preheat the grill to low.

3. Rinse and pat dry the ribs with paper towels and set them on a stable surface.

4. Combine the sugar and seasonings into a jar or bottle and shake thoroughly.

5. Rub the spice mix over the ribs, covering the meat thoroughly.

6. Place the ribs directly on the grate.

7. Baste the ribs with the sauce.

8. Cook for 2 hours, rotating the meat every 30 minutes to expose the different edges evenly to the hot side of the fire.

9. Each time you rotate the ribs, baste them with more savory sauce.

10. After 2 hours, baste the ribs with sauce one last time and wrap them in aluminum foil.

11. Place the foil pack back onto the grill and cook for another 45 minutes.

12. Remove from heat and let stand for 5 minutes before removing from foil pack.

13. Serve immediately.

Sugar and spice make this reverse cowgirl rib eye real naughty. The blend of brown sugar, salt, paprika, and other spices makes an easy, flavor-packed dry rub that you'll sensually massage all over your big ol' hunks of meat. Requiring only a few minutes on the grill (based on your cooking preferences), this rib eye is an easy and impressive dinner for a special occasion or to elevate any normal weeknight at home.

**GRILL: CHARCOAL, IDEALLY | PREP TIME: 5 MINUTES |
COOK TIME: 6 TO 15 MINUTES | MAKES: 4 SERVINGS**

4 rib eye steaks, about ½ pound each

4 tablespoons light brown sugar, packed

1 teaspoon salt

2 teaspoons ground black pepper

1 teaspoon paprika

3 cloves garlic, minced

2 teaspoons onion powder

1 teaspoon celery seed

2 teaspoons ground cumin

1 teaspoon ground coriander

olive oil cooking spray

4 to 6 sprigs fresh rosemary, for garnish

INSTRUCTIONS

1. Preheat your grill to medium-high (360–400 °F).

2. Rinse the steaks and pat dry with a paper towel. Set aside.

3. Combine the brown sugar and all the seasonings in a jar or bowl and mix thoroughly until well incorporated.

4. Lightly mist the steaks on all sides with the cooking spray.

5. With passion, rub the sugar and spice mix into the meat.

6. Place the steaks on the grill and in a quickie fashion, cook for 3 to 5 minutes, or until golden brown and slightly charred.

7. Using tongs or a spatula, reverse-cowgirl flip the steaks and cook again. For medium-rare, cook for 3 to 5 minutes. For medium, cook for 5 to 7 minutes. For medium-well, cook for 8 to 10 minutes.

8. Remove from the heat , let stand for 2 minutes, garnish with fresh rosemary, and serve.

CHERRY-POPPIN' BEEF
(CHERRY-MARINATED MEAT)

Savory, sweet, and rich. I'm talking about this cherry-marinated steak, Barb, not your third husband. The cherries, rosemary, thyme, and balsamic vinegar add complexity and texture to the beef. It's everything you could ever want from a meaty meal—or your future ex-boyfriend.

GRILL: ANY GRILL | PREP TIME: 5 TO 7 MINUTES | CHILL TIME: 4 TO 8 HOURS | COOK TIME: 6 TO 10 MINUTES | MAKES: 4 SERVINGS

2 pounds sirloin or top round steak, thinly sliced

1 (15-ounce) can dark, sweet cherries in heavy syrup

1 tablespoon olive oil

¼ cup sugar

1½ teaspoons dried thyme

1½ teaspoons dried rosemary

1 teaspoon salt

2 tablespoons balsamic vinegar

2 teaspoons garlic powder

2 teaspoons black pepper

INSTRUCTIONS

1. Rinse the beef thoroughly and pat dry with a paper towel. Place in a ziplock bag.

2. Add a full can of seductive cherries and syrup to the bag.

3. Add the oil, sugar, and seasonings to the bag and seal tightly.

4. Shake the bag until all the ingredients are thoroughly combined and the meat is glazed with the juices.

5. Open the bag, let out most of the air, and reseal. Fold the bag in half, tightening the liquid around the meat, and refrigerate for 4 to 8 hours or more.

6. When you're ready to cook, preheat the grill to medium-high.

7. On a baking tray, place two layers of aluminum foil.

8. Remove the cherries with a little bit of the marinade and put onto the foil. Wrap tightly to keep the fluids from spilling and place the foil onto the grill, directly over the flames.

9. Next, place the meat on the grill.

10. Cook for 3 to 5 minutes, until the meat starts to char and turn slightly golden.

11. Flip the meat and cook for another 2 to 3 minutes.

12. Remove the meat and cherries from the grill.

13. Plate the meat, then spoon out the cherries and any remaining liquid onto the meat.

14. Serve immediately to lose your cherry-marinated-steak virginity.

This dish utilizes an easy preparation method to create a satisfying flank steak that will leave you begging for a second taste. Fire up a gas or charcoal grill, and you'll have a sizzling hot piece of meat served up on your plate within minutes. Now the question is, what will you have on the side?

GRILL: GAS OR CHARCOAL | PREP TIME: 1 HOUR |
CHILL TIME: OVERNIGHT | COOK TIME: 10 MINUTES | MAKES: 4 SERVINGS

2 pounds flank steak

juice of 2 oranges

juice of 1 lemon

3 cloves garlic, pressed

2 tablespoons apple cider vinegar

¼ cup soy sauce

2 tablespoons honey

1 teaspoon dried minced onion

1½ teaspoons dried cilantro

1 teaspoon lemon pepper

INSTRUCTIONS

1. Get handsy with your raw meat—in a safe, hygienic manner, of course. Rinse and pat dry the steaks, then cut a few slits into each steak.

2. Package your meat by placing the steaks in a 1-gallon ziplock bag.

3. Combine the remaining ingredients in the ziplock bag with the steaks. Massage the marinade into the steaks until they are thoroughly covered and dripping with juice.

4. Press the air out of the bag and fold the bag in half.

5. Marinate overnight in the refrigerator.

6. Preheat the grill to a steamy-hot 400°F.

7. When the grill is sweltering and ready, place the steaks on the sizzling grill and cook for a quickie 5 minutes.

8. Flip the steaks and cook for another quickie 5 minutes.

9. Serve immediately to enjoy the juiciest meat.

You really have to beat this meat to get the jerky just right. An insider's tip to successfully drying out this meat is to know what cut of beef to buy. A good ol' flank steak is going to cost a bit more, but it's a leaner cut, which will make for a tastier, chewier stick of meat—if that's the way you like it.

GRILL: CHARCOAL GRILL OR SMOKER | PREP TIME: 10 MINUTES | CHILL TIME: OVERNIGHT | COOK TIME: 5 TO 8 HOURS | MAKES: 5 TO 6 SERVINGS

2 pounds thinly sliced beef

½ cup orange juice

1 cup teriyaki sauce

4 teaspoons garlic powder

4 teaspoons onion powder

½ cup brown sugar, packed

2 tablespoons sesame oil

2 tablespoons sesame seeds

2 tablespoons unseasoned rice vinegar

2 teaspoons ground ginger

1 teaspoon salt

2 teaspoons black pepper

2 handfuls of apple or peach wood chips for smoking

INSTRUCTIONS

1. Cut the beef into strips or squares about two-thirds larger than you want the jerky to wind up. Shrinkage is real.

2. Place the meat in a ziplock bag.

3. Add the other ingredients to the bag with the meat, seal the bag, and shake thoroughly until the meat is well coated.

4. Open the bag to release the air, then reseal it and fold it in half. Refrigerate overnight.

5. When you're ready to make the jerky, preheat the grill to low, adding the smoking wood chips before it reaches temperature.

6. When there's no more white smoke and the coal is ashy, place the strips of meat on the grate, away from any visible flame or glowing embers. Cover the grill.

7. Let the meat cook low and slow (my favorite) until dry, for the next 5 to 8 hours, checking every 1½ to 2 hours to make sure the embers are still going but not cooking the meat with flame, to avoid charring or overcooking the meat.

8. When the meat no longer shows any signs of redness and has become pliable (enough to bend in half without breaking), remove it from the grill and let it cool completely before eating. You just jerked your beef.

9. Store it in an air-tight container.

This recipe comes from my dear friend and Italian Stallion Lorenzo Grandipalle. He's known for having the biggest balls in town—both literally and figuratively. I swear, I can't fit even one of his savory balls in my mouth. They're that huge! Make the recipe below and let me know the number of balls you're able to house in that big, dirty mouth of yours.

GRILL: CHARCOAL, IDEALLY | PREP TIME: 10 MINUTES | COOK TIME: 8 MINUTES | MAKES: 12 TO 14 MEATBALLS

1 pound lean ground beef

1 teaspoon ground cumin

½ teaspoon ground mustard

1 teaspoon Italian seasoning

2 teaspoons dried minced onion

1 teaspoon garlic powder

½ teaspoon ground black pepper

1 teaspoon chili powder

½ teaspoon paprika

olive oil

INSTRUCTIONS

1. Preheat the grill to medium.

2. Combine the meat and all the spices in a bowl, mixing until everything is well incorporated.

3. Remove overflowing tablespoons, approximately, of the meat mixture and shape it into balls with your hands. Your ball size is up to you. Set them on a plate.

4. Brush a light layer of olive oil on all sides of each meatball.

5. Place the meatballs on the grill, away from the flame, and cook for 2 minutes.

6. Move the meatballs onto another side and cook for another 2 minutes.

7. Repeat until the meatballs are browned on all sides.

8. Serve immediately with your favorite BBQ sauce, or straight up.

Let the record (er, this book) show that you can put any filling you want into a tortilla (hard or soft, your choice!) and call it a tasty taco. This recipe is a classic meat-stuffed taco, featuring juicy ground beef. But if you're not in the mood for beef, go for cock. Or pork it up. Or try seafood. The taco is the ultimate vehicle for shoveling delicious meat into your mouth without the guilt or shame.

GRILL: CHARCOAL | PREP TIME: 10 MINUTES | COOK TIME: 30 MINUTES | MAKES: 8 TO 10 TACOS

TACO SEASONING

1 tablespoon chili powder

1 teaspoon garlic powder

1 teaspoon onion powder

½ teaspoon crushed red pepper

½ teaspoon paprika

2 teaspoons ground cumin

1 teaspoon ground black pepper

1 teaspoon salt, optional

TACOS

handful of mesquite wood chips for smoking

1 pound lean ground beef

2 cloves garlic, minced

¼ white onion, thinly sliced

4 tablespoons taco seasoning

8 to 10 soft tortillas or crunchy taco shells

4 cups shredded lettuce

1 tomato, diced

¼ red onion, thinly sliced

1 cup salsa

other chopped/sliced veggies, as desired

INSTRUCTIONS

1. Before lighting your charcoal, spread a handful of mesquite wood chips for smoking throughout the grill.

2. Preheat the grill to medium-high and cover.

3. Line a baking sheet with two layers of aluminum foil large enough to wrap around the meat and cover it tightly.

4. Lay the fresh ground meat onto the foil, then sprinkle the taco seasoning over the meat.

5. Add the white onion.

6. Stir it all together using your hands or a wooden spoon, then, then seal the pack.

7. Place the pack on the grill and cover.

8. Cook for 30 minutes.

9. Remove the foil pack from the heat. With caution, peel back the opening and let the steam out for a couple of minutes before serving.

10. If using soft taco shells, warm them in the microwave on a flat plate for 30 seconds to 1 minute.

11. Serve the meat in the shells with the veggies and salsa and other preferred toppings.

There's no parking the beef bus in Tuna Town here. This beef patty is going straight for Bunsville. Let this meat sandwich slide right into your sexy, salivating mouth. We won't judge if you go back for seconds, thirds, fourths, and fifths.

GRILL: ANY GRILL | PREP TIME: 7 TO 10 MINUTES | COOK TIME: 6 TO 8 MINUTES | MAKES: 6 TO 8 SLIDERS

1 pound lean ground beef

2 cloves garlic, minced

¼ white onion, finely chopped

½ teaspoon dried thyme

½ teaspoon dried rosemary

1 teaspoon Italian seasoning

¼ teaspoon ground mustard

½ teaspoon ground cumin

½ teaspoon ground black pepper

½ teaspoon salt

6 to 8 mini buns

toppings (cheese, lettuces, tomato), as desired

condiments (mustard, relish, ketchup, horseradish sauce), as desired

INSTRUCTIONS

1. Preheat the grill to medium-high.

2. Combine the meat, garlic, onion, and seasonings in a bowl. Mix with your hands or a fork until thoroughly combined.

3. Shape equal portions of the meat mixture into small disks and lay out on a pan or plate.

4. Lightly brush the grill with oil to prevent the meat from sticking.

5. Carefully place the disks of meat onto the grill and cook for 4 to 5 minutes.

6. Flip the meat and cook on the other side for an additional 3 to 5 minutes or until the meat is golden brown and lightly charred on both sides.

7. Remove the meat from the grill immediately and serve up on mini buns with condiments of your choosing.

BANGIN' PLUMP RUMP ROAST

My mom's incredible, perfect, plump rump (roast) is one for the ages. Every special childhood memory of mine includes her juicy roast. My dad would lose his mind when he'd see her preparing her savory rump for him. It eventually became a weekly tradition, and Mom would serve it every Sunday. Everyone in our family would be so utterly satisfied with this bangin' meat on the table. Now, thinking back to those family dinners, I recall Mom sending us kids to bed pretty early while she and Dad had dessert at the table. From my room, I'd hear her moan, "How is it, Daddy?"

GRILL: GAS | PREP TIME: 22 MINUTES | CHILL TIME: OVERNIGHT |
COOK TIME: 16 TO 20 MINUTES + 1½ TO 2 HOURS | MAKES: 8 TO 12 SERVINGS

¼ cup red wine

¼ cup orange juice

3 tablespoons olive oil

juice of 1 lemon

¼ cup honey

2 tablespoons Dijon mustard

3 tablespoons teriyaki sauce

6 cloves garlic, minced

2 teaspoons dried thyme

2 teaspoons Worcestershire sauce

½ teaspoon salt

½ teaspoon ground black pepper

4 pounds rump roast

INSTRUCTIONS

1. Combine all the ingredients, in order, except the meat, in a ziplock bag.

2. Seal the bag and shake it up until all the ingredients are thoroughly combined.

3. Open the bag, place the meat in, and reseal the bag, letting most of the air out. Massage the marinade into the meat and refrigerate overnight to let it rest.

4. Preheat the grill to high for 15 minutes.

5. Place a drip pan in the grill, then put the meat over the direct heat.

6. Sear the meat on each side for a quick 4 to 5 minutes each.

7. When the meat has been seared reduce the heat to medium-high.

8. Cover the grill and let the roast cook for 1 hour and 15 minutes for medium-rare, 1½ hours for medium, or 2 hours for well done.

9. Check the internal temperature every 15 to 20 minutes. It is done when it reaches 135-140 °F.

10. Remove the meat from the grill and let it stand for 15 minutes before carving.

11. Carve and serve.

The beautiful, marbled fat. The rich, juicy, tender meat. This red-hot rib roast is a marvelous feast for your eyes, your mouth, your belly, and your soul.

GRILL: ANY GRILL | PREP TIME: 10 MINUTES |
COOK TIME: 3 TO 4 HOURS | MAKES: 8 TO 12 SERVINGS

2 tablespoons olive oil

8 cloves garlic, minced

2 teaspoons salt

2 teaspoons ground black pepper

2 tablespoons dried thyme

2 tablespoons dried basil

2 tablespoons dried sage

1 tablespoon dried rosemary

2 tablespoons paprika

1 standing rib roast (about 6 ribs)

INSTRUCTIONS

1. Prepare the grill for indirect grilling by place a large dripping pan under the grate.

2. Preheat the grill to 375°F. (Or see grill chart on page 120.)

3. Combine all the seasonings in a jar. Shake thoroughly until completely combined.

4. Rinse the roast and pat it dry with paper towels.

5. Brush olive oil over the roast and then rub in the spice mix, thoroughly coating all sides of the roast.

6. Oil the grill grate and place the meat over the drip pan.

7. Be sure to add a few tablespoons of water to the drip pan to help create a gravy.

8. Cook the roast for 12 to 14 minutes per each pound of meat, 3 to 4 hours for the full roast. The internal temperature should be 120°F.

9. Rotate the roast every 15 to 20 minutes and brush it lightly with olive oil to help keep the meat oh-so-moist.

10. When the roast is done cooking, remove it from the heat and let it stand for 10 minutes before serving.

Whoever said size doesn't matter clearly hasn't realized the importance of length. No one enjoys short, dry beef sticks. The key to these extra-long moist beef sticks is soaking your meat chunks in a flavor-packed marinade for at least 8 hours. The longer the meat is immersed in the mouthwatering marinade, the more pleasure you'll experience when you finally take a bite of this beef.

GRILL: GAS OR CHARCOAL | PREP TIME: 25 MINUTES | CHILL TIME: 8 TO 12 HOURS | COOK TIME: 8 TO 10 MINUTES | MAKES: 10 TO 12 KEBABS

MARINADE

¼ cup soy sauce

1 teaspoon Worcestershire sauce

juice of 1 lime

juice of 1 lemon

1 tablespoon white vinegar

2 tablespoons olive oil

1 teaspoon dried rosemary, crushed

½ teaspoon ground black pepper

2 teaspoons dried minced onion

1 teaspoon garlic powder

½ teaspoon dried parsley flakes

KEBABS

1½ pounds stew beef chunks

2 red peppers, cut into 10 to 12 chunks

2 green peppers, cut into 10 to 12 chunks

2 yellow peppers, cut into 10 to 12 chunks

1 red onion, cut into 10 to 12 chunks

INSTRUCTIONS

1. Make the juice by combining all the marinade ingredients in a 1-gallon ziplock bag.

2. Add the stew beef chunks to the bag with the marinade.

3. Tenderly massage beef and marinade together until the meat is completely coated and soaked in juice.

4. Squeeze air out of the bag and seal it tightly. Fold the bag and place it in the refrigerator.

5. Chill for 8 to 12 hours. Soak that meat real good.

6. Preheat the grill to medium heat. (Don't worry; things get hotter once the beef is in your mouth.)

7. Pierce one chunk of wet, marinated meat with a stiff metal or bamboo shish kebab skewer.

8. Add the veggies and more meat until each skewer is stuffed full.

9. Lay out the kebabs onto the grill, not touching each other. Each meat stick needs its space.

10. Cook for 4 to 5 minutes.

11. Flip the kebabs and grill on the other side for an additional 4 to 5 minutes.

Let me introduce you to the tantric sex of grilling. Tantric sex is a slow form of intercourse that increases intimacy and builds an intensified mind-body connection that can lead to mind-blowing orgasms. This brisket will do the same.

GRILL: CHARCOAL | PREP TIME: 10 MINUTES | CHILL TIME: 4 HOURS |
COOK TIME: 7 TO 8 HOURS + 26 TO 28 MINUTES | MAKES: 6 TO 8 SERVINGS

BRISKET

1 tablespoon coarse salt

1 tablespoon chili powder

1 tablespoon sugar

1½ teaspoons ground black pepper

1 teaspoon ground cumin

1 teaspoon dried cilantro

1 teaspoon yellow curry powder

2 cups hickory or mesquite wood chips for smoking

5 to 6 pounds beef brisket, with ¼- to ½-inch-thick layer of fat

BBQ SAUCE

1 tablespoon butter

1 small red onion, minced

4 cloves garlic, minced

1 cup ketchup

¼ cup dark brown sugar, packed

¼ cup lemon juice

3 tablespoons apple cider vinegar

3 tablespoons tomato paste

1½ tablespoons yellow mustard

1 tablespoon Worcestershire sauce

1 tablespoon chili powder

2 teaspoons smoked paprika

TO MAKE THE BRISKET

1. Combine all the seasonings in a jar and shake vigorously.

2. Rinse the brisket and pat dry with paper towels.

3. Pour out the seasoning mix onto the meat and rub it into the meat with your hands. Make sure to cover all sides of the meat, including the fatty side.

4. Wrap the meat in plastic wrap or foil and refrigerate for 4 hours to cure.

5. When the meat has cured, preheat the grill to low, adding the smoking wood chips as you get the fire going. Let the smoke completely stop piping white before adding the meat.

6. Place the brisket, fat side down, into an aluminum foil pan.

7. Cover the meat with BBQ sauce.

8. Place the pan in the center of the grate, away from the heat, and cover the grill.

9. Smoke the meat until it's tender—for 7 to 8 hours.

10. Every 90 minutes or so, baste the brisket with more BBQ sauce and the fat juices in the pan.

11. Add fresh coals and fresh wood chips every 2 hours to keep the heat and flavorful smoke going. Be sure to avoid stoking the flames too high, though, and maintain that low heat level.

TO MAKE THE BBQ SAUCE

1. In a large saucepan, heat the butter over medium heat.

2. When the butter has melted, 1 to 2 minutes, add the onion.

3. Cook, stirring constantly, for 2 to 3 minutes or until the onions are tender.

12. After the meat has cooked for 7 to 8 hours, it should be falling apart and tender. When it's reached this stage, remove the pan from the grill and let it rest for 15 minutes.

13. Transfer the meat to a cutting board or serving tray and thinly slice it across the grain.

14. Serve and enjoy with more BBQ sauce or as is.

4. Add the garlic and cook for 1 minute more.

5. Next, add the rest of the ingredients and bring to a boil.

6. Reduce the heat to low and leave the saucepan uncovered to simmer for 20 minutes.

LET'S GET PORKIN'

This porker likes it rough, stuffed, and tied-up. Take control of your meat and show it who's boss by using butcher twine to keep it tied up while it cooks. It sounds harder than it is. When the meat is cooked, you can impress your dinner guests with your hard work in the kitchen. But secretly, you'll revel in the knowledge that the pork preparation was the easiest you've ever had.

GRILL: ANY GRILL | PREP TIME: 7 TO 10 MINUTES | COOK TIME: 1 HOUR 45 MINUTES | MAKES: 4 SERVINGS

½ teaspoons salt

½ teaspoon ground black pepper

2 teaspoons paprika

2 teaspoons garlic powder

2 teaspoons onion powder

2 teaspoons chili powder

¼ cup brown sugar, packed

2 pounds pork tenderloin (usually 2 tenderloins)

1 cup BBQ sauce of your choice

INSTRUCTIONS

1. Combine the seasonings in a jar and shake thoroughly.

2. Rinse the pork and pat it dry with paper towels.

3. Use butcher twine to tie up the meat to keep the shape. To do this, simply place the tenderloins together and work down the meat, tying knots.

4. Now massage the spice mix rub into the pork loin.

5. Preheat the grill to medium-high heat. Prepare the grill for indirect grilling by place a dripping pan under the grate.

6. Lightly oil the grate with olive oil and place the tenderloin on the grate over the dripping pan.

7. Cook for 30 minutes, turning the meat over once.

8. Brush BBQ sauce on the tenderloin and cook for another 1 hour 15 minutes, flipping the meat twice and basting again with more BBQ sauce.

9. The internal temperature should reach 145°F by this point. When it has, remove from the heat and let stand for 10 minutes before slicing and serving with additional BBQ sauce.

DOWN WITH BUTT STUFF (PORK BUTT)

This booty demands your undivided attention for a few hours. You'll need to check the meat on the grill in 15-minute intervals to make sure you keep that baby moist.

GRILL: CHARCOAL | PREP TIME: 7 TO 10 MINUTES | CHILL TIME: 4 HOURS + 1 HOUR | REST TIME: 4 HOURS | COOK TIME: 6 HOURS | MAKES: 6 TO 8 SERVINGS

2 cups mesquite, hickory, or apple wood chips for smoking

1 (4-pound) pork butt

4 tablespoons brown sugar, packed

1 tablespoon paprika

2 teaspoons salt

2 teaspoons ground cumin

2 teaspoons chili powder

2 teaspoons ground black pepper

1 tablespoon garlic powder

1 tablespoon onion powder

1 teaspoon dried sage

2 cups BBQ sauce of choice

INSTRUCTIONS

1. Soak the wood chips for 4 hours.

2. Preheat the grill to low, approximately 225°F, with charcoal on half of the grill and a pan full of water under the other half.

3. Rinse the pork, then pat it dry with paper towels. Set aside.

4. Combine rub ingredients in jar or bottle and shake thoroughly to incorporate.

5. Passionately rub the spice mix all over the meat and place it on the grill over the water pan, fat side up.

6. Cover the grill and cook the butt for 5 hours, until the internal temperature reaches 145°F.

7. Uncover the grill and brush BBQ sauce on the meat. Cook for another 15 minutes.

8. Repeat the basting process again every 15 minutes, rotating the meat, for four times total.

9. The meat should have an internal temperature of 145°F in the middle of the roast.

10. Remove the roast from the grill and wrap it tightly in foil. Let it stand for 1 hour before shredding and serving.

I love a big ol' sausage, don't you? Here, you'll get to enjoy six of 'em. It's up to you if you want to share the bratwursts or keep it a huge private sausage party for one.

GRILL: GAS, IDEALLY | PREP TIME: 5 MINUTES | COOK TIME: 20 MINUTES + 15 MINUTES | MAKES: 6 SERVINGS

6 bratwursts, raw

1 pound frozen sweet potato fries, thawed

1 bell pepper, sliced

½ red onion, sliced

¼ cup olive oil

2 teaspoons onion powder

2 teaspoons garlic powder

1 tablespoon dried parsley flakes

INSTRUCTIONS

1. Preheat the grill to medium.

2. Place the sausages on the grate. Cook for 10 minutes.

3. On the other end of the grill, place a cast-iron skillet to preheat.

4. Combine the fries, bell pepper, onion, oil, and spices in a ziplock bag. Seal the bag and vigorously shake it, thoroughly coating the veggies with the oil and spices.

5. When the pan is smoking hot, put the pepper and onion mix into the pan. Stir regularly to keep the veggies from sticking and burning.

6. Using tongs, flip the sausages and cook for another 7 to 10 minutes.

7. Insert a meat thermometer and verify that the sausages have reached 160°F internal temperature.

8. After the sausages are cooked, remove them from the heat. Cut them up into slices and toss them together with the veggie mix.

9. Serve immediately.

Why two-fingered, you ask? Because the meat should be at least two fingers thick. What did you think I meant? [Unintelligible response.] Oh, wow. That took an unexpected turn.

**GRILL: ANY GRILL | PREP TIME: 7 TO 10 MINUTES |
COOK TIME: 10 TO 16 MINUTES | MAKES: 4 CHOPS**

CHOPS

4 thick pork chops

3 tablespoons brown sugar, packed

½ teaspoon salt

½ teaspoon ground black pepper

1 teaspoon paprika

½ teaspoon ground mustard

1 teaspoon onion powder

1 teaspoon garlic powder

olive oil for grill

SAUCE

⅓ cup apple cider vinegar

½ cup brown sugar, packed

1 cup ketchup

1½ teaspoons Worcestershire sauce

1 teaspoon garlic powder

1 teaspoon onion powder

¼ cup honey

INSTRUCTIONS

1. Preheat the grill to 400°F.

2. Rinse the pork chops and pat them dry with a paper towel. Set aside.

3. In a jar or bottle, combine all the ingredients for the rub and shake together until fully incorporated.

4. Rub the spice mix over the pork chops, covering all sides.

5. Brush the grill lightly with oil, then place the chops on the grate. Cook for 5 to 8 minutes, until char marks form.

6. While the meat is cooking, pour all the ingredients for the sauce into a small saucepan. Cook over medium-high heat while stirring for 2 minutes.

7. Reduce heat to medium and cook for 2 minutes more. Remove the pan from the heat and set it aside.

8. Flip the chops and grill them for 5 to 8 minutes more, until the internal temperature reaches 145°F.

9. Top the chops with the sauce and serve immediately.

One bite of this pork and you'll be dripping wet—because you'll be salivating.

**GRILL: ANY GRILL | PREP TIME: 5 MINUTES |
COOK TIME: 16 MINUTES | MAKES: 4 SERVINGS**

PORK CHOPS

1 cup brown sugar, packed

juice of 1 lemon

2 tablespoons honey

1 (15-16-ounce) can peaches with syrup

4 boneless pork chops

CREAM

1 (8-ounce) package cream cheese, softened

2 tablespoons honey

¼ cup chopped pecans

¼ cup heavy cream

INSTRUCTIONS

1. Preheat the grill to high.

2. Lightly oil a large cast-iron skillet or grill pan and place it on the grill to preheat.

3. In a medium mixing bowl, combine the brown sugar, lemon juice, honey, and peaches with the syrup. Stir until thoroughly combined.

4. Place pork chops in the skillet. Sear the meat on both sides for 3 to 4 minutes on each side.

5. Add the peach mixture, stirring constantly, while ladling it over the chops.

6. Continue cooking the chops, flipping them every 3 to 4 minutes and continuing to ladle the sauce over the meat.

7. Cook for a total of 16 minutes or until the meat reaches an internal temperature of 145°F.

8. Remove the pan from the grill and let it stand for 5 minutes.

9. While the pork is standing, combine the ingredients for the cream mixture until it is thick and smooth.

10. Plate the chops, spooning the peach sauce evenly over the pork.

11. Top with the cream mixture and serve.

FALL-OFF-THE-BONE
DRY-RUBBED RIBS

Seasoned with a homemade dry rub and grilled until tender, these ribs will melt in your mouth as they fall off the hard bone. Slathered in a homemade BBQ sauce, these ribs will have you licking every one of your fingers for every last drop of dirty deliciousness.

GRILL: CHARCOAL | PREP TIME: 20 MINUTES |
COOK TIME: 3 HOURS | MAKES: 12 TO 16 RIBS

BBQ SAUCE

1 (15-ounce) can tomato sauce

2 tablespoons apple cider vinegar

1 (6-ounce) can tomato paste

½ cup apple juice

½ cup brown sugar, packed

4 teaspoons ground mustard

1 tablespoon garlic powder

2 teaspoons onion powder

4 teaspoons Worcestershire sauce

2 teaspoons salt

2 teaspoons ground black pepper

2 teaspoons chili powder

1 teaspoon celery seed

RIBS

2 handfuls of apple wood chips for smoking

1½ to 2 pounds ribs

3 tablespoons sugar

1 teaspoon paprika

1 teaspoon ground mustard

1 teaspoon ground black pepper

1 teaspoon salt

2 teaspoons garlic powder

1 teaspoon chili powder

2 teaspoons ground cumin

1 teaspoon dried thyme

1 teaspoon onion powder

olive oil

TO MAKE THE BBQ SAUCE

1. Combine all the ingredients in a medium saucepan over medium heat.

2. Stir the ingredients until thoroughly incorporated, for 2 minutes.

3. Reduce the heat to medium-low and let it simmer for 10 minutes.

4. Remove the saucepan from the heat and set it aside.

TO MAKE THE RIBS

1. Add 2 handfuls of apple wood chips to the charcoal grill.

2. Preheat the grill to medium-low and cover.

3. Rinse the ribs and pat them dry with a paper towel.

4. Combine sugar and spices in a jar or bottle and shake well until all the ingredients are thoroughly incorporated.

5. Heavily coat the ribs with olive oil.

6. Pour half of the spice mix onto the ribs and rub it into the meat.

7. Flip the meat and rub the second half of the seasoning mix into the meat, thoroughly coating it on all sides, front and back.

8. Place the meat on the grill, away from the fire.

9. Baste the ribs with the BBQ sauce and cook for 30 minutes.

10. Flip the meat and baste again with more BBQ sauce.

11. Cook for another 2½ hours, flipping and re-basting every 30 minutes.

12. When meat has reached an internal temperature of 145°F, baste each side one last time and cook for 10 minutes on each side.

13. Remove the rack from the heat and let it stand for 2 to 3 minutes before cutting into individual ribs and serving.

This rack likes to go au naturel. It doesn't ask for much, just a simple seasoning blend and a bit of oil to stay moist. This spice mix is both sweet and savory, delivering a rack you've only seen in your dreams.

GRILL: CHARCOAL | PREP TIME: 10 MINUTES | COOK TIME: 2¹/₂ | HOURS | MAKES: 12 TO 16 RIBS

2 handfuls of apple or mesquite wood chips for smoking

1 rack of ribs

4 tablespoons sugar

2 teaspoon salt

2 teaspoon ground mustard

4 teaspoons garlic powder

2 teaspoons onion powder

2 tablespoons ground cumin

2 teaspoons celery seed

2 teaspoons ground black pepper

2 teaspoons ground coriander

½ to ⅔ cup olive oil

INSTRUCTIONS

1. Preheat the grill to medium-high.

2. Rinse the ribs and pat them dry with a paper towel.

3. Combine the sugar and spices in a jar or bottle and shake well until thoroughly incorporated.

4. Brush oil heavily on all sides of the ribs.

5. Pour out half of the rub onto the ribs and rub it into the meat.

6. Flip the rack of ribs over and pour out the second half of the rub, working it into the meat.

7. Oil the grill with olive oil or vegetable oil and place the rack of ribs onto the grill away from the flames.

8. Cover the grill.

9. Rotate the rack of ribs every 30 minutes for 2½ hours, exposing all sides to the hottest part of the grill.

10. If the ribs are getting dried out, gently brush them with more oil.

11. After the ribs have reached an internal temperature of 145°F and the meat is tender and falling off the bone, remove the rack from the heat.

12. Let it stand for 3 to 5 minutes before cutting into individual ribs and serving with your BBQ sauce of choice.

FORBIDDEN FRUIT-GLAZED RIBS (APPLE-GLAZED BABY BACK RIBS)

Using the forbidden fruit to create a more complex flavor profile makes these ribs so bad they're good. The finger-licking glazed rack will leave you sticky, dirty, and satisfied as you thank God for the mind-blowing culinary affair you just experienced.

GRILL: ANY GRILL | PREP TIME: 12 TO 15 MINUTES | COOK TIME: 3 HOURS | MAKES: 4 TO 5 SERVINGS

4 pounds baby back ribs

3 cups apple cider

½ cup dark brown sugar, packed

¼ teaspoon white pepper

pinch of salt

1 tablespoon garlic powder

¼ teaspoon ground mustard

½ cup apple cider vinegar

1 cup applesauce

¼ cup honey

1 small white onion, thinly sliced

1 cup BBQ sauce

INSTRUCTIONS

1. Preheat the grill to medium-low.

2. Rinse the ribs and pat them dry with paper towels.

3. Remove the membrane from the underside of the ribs by sliding a clean screwdriver along each bone and under the end of the membrane to loosen. Grab the membrane with a paper towel and pull it off. Set the ribs aside.

4. Pour apple cider into a disposable foil pan large enough to hold the ribs.

5. Sprinkle the sugar and the four seasonings evenly over the cider in the pan.

6. Pour in the vinegar next, then ladle in the applesauce.

7. Mix everything together in the pan, then add the ribs.

8. Drizzle the honey over the ribs, then sprinkle the onion into the pan.

9. Now ladle the glaze over the ribs in the pan.

10. Place the pan on the grill and cover the grill. Cook for 30 minutes.

11. Uncover the grill. Turn the ribs over and ladle the glaze over the ribs again. Cook for another 30 minutes.

12. Remove the ribs from the pan and place directly over the flame, bone side up. Brush the glaze over the ribs and cook for 10 minutes.

13. Turn the ribs over and brush more glaze over the ribs. Cook for another 10 minutes.

14. Stoke the fire to bring it to medium-high heat.

15. Cook for another 1½ hours, flipping the ribs every 20 minutes or so, brushing more glaze over the ribs each time.

16. The meat should be peeling back slightly from the bone at this stage. This is how you can tell the meat is done.

17. Remove it from the grill. Stir the remaining glaze and brush it over ribs one last time. Cover with foil and let stand for 10 minutes.

18. Cut between the bones and serve.

There are no shortcuts when it comes to good and tender pork. To get the meat just right takes time. This is no 'wham-bam, thank you, ma'am' sort of situation. The pork needs your tender, loving care as its roasts to reach the perfect pull-apart texture. Then, you can stuff your face with this juicy meat on buns as soft as clouds.

GRILL: CHARCOAL WITH WOOD CHUNKS | PREP TIME: 7 MINUTES | COOK TIME: 4 HOURS | MAKES: 12 TO 14 SANDWICHES

PORK

2 handfuls cherry wood chips for smoking

2 handfuls apple wood chips for smoking

2½ pounds pork loin

pulled-pork rub

1 large red onion, thinly sliced

BBQ sauce

PORK RUB

3 tablespoons granulated sugar

½ tablespoon garlic powder

½ tablespoon chili powder

1 teaspoon salt

½ tablespoon ground cumin

1 teaspoon paprika

½ teaspoon ground black pepper

BBQ SAUCE

1 (15-ounce) can tomato sauce

1 (6-ounce) can tomato paste

⅔ cup light brown sugar, packed

¼ cup apple cider vinegar

1 tablespoon Worcestershire sauce

¼ teaspoon ground black pepper

1 teaspoon paprika

2 teaspoons garlic powder

1 teaspoon onion powder

½ teaspoon cayenne pepper

½ teaspoon salt

TO SERVE

12 to 14 buns

PORK

1. Load your grill with charcoal as usual.

2. Add 2 handfuls of cherry wood chips for smoking.

3. Add 2 handful of apple wood chips for smoking.

4. Bring the temperature to medium-low and cover the grill.

5. While the grill is heating up, line a rimmed baking sheet with two layers of aluminum foil.

6. Rinse the pork loin and pat it dry with paper towels. Place the meat on the lined baking sheet.

7. Combine rub ingredients in a jar and shake to combine.

8. Intimately rub the seasoning mix on all sides of the loin, including the fatty side.

9. Add the sliced red onion, spreading them throughout the foil pack.

10. Wrap the pork and onion up tightly in the foil, adding more layers of foil, if necessary, to keep the fluids from dripping and making a mess while it cooks.

11. Place the foil pack on the grill and cover. Cook for 4 hours.

12. Check the embers about once an hour, making sure there are still glowing embers until at least the last half hour of cooking. Keep the grill covered for the full 4 hours.

13. After 4 hours, peel back the foil and check the internal temperature. The pork should give an instant read of 145°F.

14. If the temperature is right, use a fork to see if you can pull the meat easily. It should be falling apart easily at this stage.

15. When the meat reaches this texture, remove it from the heat and let it stand for 10 minutes before removing the foil.

16. Remove the foil, pull the pork apart with a fork, and serve it on soft whole wheat buns, topped with the BBQ sauce.

BBQ SAUCE

1. Combine all the ingredients in a medium saucepan.

2. Bring the heat to medium-high.

3. Stir consistently for 2 minutes, then let the sauce rest until it begins to boil, about 4 minutes.

4. When the sauce boils, reduce the heat to low and let it simmer for 15 minutes.

5. Remove the pan from the heat and let it cool for 5 minutes, then serv in soft buns.

PORK THREE TANTALIZING WAYS: CARVED, SHREDDED, OR PULLED

Don't wait—you're going to want to fork with this recipe immediately. No matter which way you slice the succulent, tender pork, the use of both cherry and apple wood chips makes this tender loin a total smoke show.

**GRILL: CHARCOAL | PREP TIME: 7 TO 10 MINUTES |
COOK TIME: 3 HOURS | MAKES: 8 TO 10 SERVINGS**

2 handfuls cherry wood chips

2 handfuls apple wood chips

2½ pounds pork loin

3 tablespoons sugar

1 teaspoon salt

1 tablespoon garlic powder

2 teaspoons dried thyme

1 teaspoon dried rosemary

2 teaspoons onion powder

2 tablespoons honey

½ cup apple juice

PULLED OR SHREDDED PORK

1. Add the cherry wood chips and apple wood chips to the grill for smoking.

2. Preheat the grill to medium-low and cover it.

3. Layer 2 sheets of aluminum foil onto a rimmed baking sheet.

4. Rinse pork loin and pat dry with a paper towel.

5. Put the pork on the foil.

6. Combine the sugar and the five spices in a jar or bottle and shake thoroughly.

7. Shake half the spice mix over the pork and gently massage it into the meat.

8. Flip the pork and rub the rest of the spice mix into the meat.

9. Drizzle the honey over the pork.

10. Drizzle the apple juice over the pork.

CARVED PORK

1. Preheat the grill to medium.

2. Prepare the meat as above.

3. Cook for 1½ hours.

11. Take another two sheets of aluminum foil and top the pork.

12. Wrap all four sheets of foil tightly around pork, preventing the apple juice from leaking out.

13. Place the meat pack onto the grill and cover it again.

14. Cook for 3 hours, stoking the embers as necessary, every hour.

15. Uncover the pork and check the temperature. When the interior temperature reaches 145°F, remove the meat from the grill.

16. Carefully remove the pork from the wrap and let it stand for 3 to 5 minutes before pulling or shredding the meat.

17. Serve hot or cold.

4. Check the internal temperature. If it has reached 145°F, remove it from the heat and let it stand for 5 minutes. If it has not, cook for another 30 minutes and test again.

5. Carefully remove the pork from the wrap.

6. Carve as desired, and serve.

PORKIN' THE TACOS
(TACOS AL PASTOR)

Holy forkin' shirt, these crave-worthy pork tacos are out of this world. When the juicy meat is almost done on the grill, these stuffed tacos will come together faster than you can say, "I want your pork in my taco."

GRILL: CHARCOAL | PREP TIME: 25 MINUTES | COOK TIME: 3 HOURS | MAKES: 10 TACOS

RUB

1 tablespoon ground cumin

1 teaspoon sea salt

2 teaspoons chili powder

1 tablespoon garlic powder

1 teaspoon onion powder

1 teaspoon celery seed

1 teaspoon dried oregano

1 teaspoon black pepper

1 teaspoon ground mustard

1 teaspoon paprika

TACOS

2 handfuls apple wood chips for smoking

1½ pounds pork loin

taco rub

juice of 2 limes

¼ fresh pineapple, cut into thin strips

1 fresh mango, cut into thin strips

2 large handfuls fresh cilantro

1 yellow or orange bell pepper

¼ red onion, thinly sliced

2 cups salsa, optional

10 flour tortillas

INSTRUCTIONS

1. Add the handfuls of apple wood chips to the charcoal and preheat to medium-low.

2. On a rimmed baking sheet, lay out two thick layers of aluminum foil.

3. Rinse the pork and pat dry with a paper towel. Lay on the aluminum foil.

4. Combine rub ingredients in a jar and shake to combine.

5. Massage the dry rub onto the meat, covering all sides. Set the remainder of the rub aside.

6. Fold the edges of the foil upward to create a bowl around the meat.

7. Drizzle lime juice over the pork, then dump the remainder of the rub into the packet.

8. Seal the packet and put it on the grill, away from the fire. Cover the grill, leaving the top vent open fully.

9. Cook for 3 hours.

10. When the meat is nearing ready, prepare the fruit, cilantro, bell pepper, and onion.

11. Check the meat after three hours. If the internal temperature has reached 145°F, it's done. If not, rewrap the packet and leave it on for 30 minutes longer, then test again. Be sure the embers are still smoldering, and smoke is still coming out of the grill.

12. When the meat is done, remove it from the grill and let it stand for 5 minutes.

13. Remove the foil. Pull the pork with two forks and serve it on tortillas with the fruit, herbs, onion, and salsa, if desired.

BACON-BOUND TATERS
(BACON-WRAPPED POTATOES)

These baby taters are flirting with bad-boy bacon. As expected, the naughty twosome is even better together. One bite and you'll find yourself on the dark side as well. Serve as an appetizer or a side dish.

**GRILL: ANY GRILL| PREP TIME: 20 TO 25 MINUTES |
COOK TIME: 30 MINUTES | MAKES: 6 SERVINGS**

2 tablespoons brown sugar, packed

2 teaspoons paprika

2 teaspoons garlic powder

1 teaspoon chili powder

½ teaspoon ground mustard

½ teaspoon celery seed

1 teaspoon dried minced onion

½ teaspoon ground black pepper

½ teaspoon salt

28 to 32 baby potatoes

2 teaspoons olive oil

1 pound raw bacon, strips cut in half

INSTRUCTIONS

1. Preheat the grill to high.

2. Put the brown sugar and eight spices in a jar and shake until thoroughly combined.

3. Rinse the potatoes thoroughly and remove any bad spots or eyes.

4. Put the potatoes into a container with the olive oil, cover with a lid, and shake until the potatoes are covered with the oil.

5. Next, add half of the seasoning to the container with potatoes. Cover and shake again, coating the potatoes with the seasoning.

6. Now dump the rest of the seasoning into a wide-mouthed bowl.

7. Dip each half strip of bacon into the seasoning, then wrap it around one potato.

8. Repeat with all of the bacon strips and potatoes. You may wish to skewer the potatoes with toothpicks to keep the bacon in place.

9. Lightly brush the grill rack with olive oil.

10. When the potatoes are coated and neatly wrapped, place them on the grill and cook for 15 minutes.

11. Flip the potatoes and cook for another 15 minutes.

12. Remove them from the grill and let stand for 3 to 5 minutes until cool enough to eat.

Sing it with me, *beanies and weenies sitting in a pan, k-i-s-s-i-n-g*. This classic dish may not be date-approved (um, beans, hello!), but it is the ultimate comfort dish, especially when you know these wieners are the only pork you'll have in your mouth tonight.

GRILL: ANY GRILL | PREP TIME: 3 TO 5 MINUTES | COOK TIME: 40 MINUTES | MAKES: 8 TO 10 SERVINGS

1 (28-ounce) can baked beans

6 slices bacon

1 white or yellow onion, sliced

⅓ cup BBQ sauce

2 tablespoons yellow mustard

1 teaspoon apple cider vinegar

¼ cup dark brown sugar, packed

½ teaspoon ground black pepper

1 teaspoon hot sauce (optional)

8 to 10 hot dogs

INSTRUCTIONS

1. Preheat the grill to medium-high, allowing for indirect heat on half the grill.

2. Combine all the ingredients, except the hot dogs, in a disposal foil pan. Stir until fully incorporated.

3. Cover the pan with foil and place on the indirect heat side of the grill.

4. Cook for 40 minutes or until the onions are tender and beans are heated all the way through.

5. After the beans have been cooking for about 25 minutes, put the hot dogs onto the grill over the flame.

6. Cook the hot dogs for 2 to 3 minutes, until sear marks begin to appear.

7. Rotate the hot dogs and cook for another 2 to 3 minutes.

8. Rotate the hot dogs again and cook on their final side for another 2 to 3 minutes.

9. Remove the hot dogs from the fire and chop into large bite-sized chunks and add them to the bean pan.

10. Cook everything for another 10 minutes.

11. Remove the pan from the heat and let it stand for 5 minutes before serving.

Remember "no glove, no weenie love"? Forget the little bite-sized pigs in a blanket. Those are for the children. This is the adult version, using full-sized wieners wrapped in deliciously flaky crescent dough, all for your personal pleasure.

GRILL: ANY GRILL | PREP TIME: 10 MINUTES | COOK TIME: 20 TO 25 MINUTES | MAKES: 8 SERVINGS

2 tablespoons poppy seeds

2 teaspoons onion powder

2 teaspoons garlic powder

1 teaspoon coarse sea salt

1 (8-ounce) can prepared crescent dough (8 rolls)

8 high-quality pork hotdogs or fully cooked brats

1 egg, whisked

¼ cup Dijon mustard

INSTRUCTIONS

1. Preheat the grill to 350°F.

2. Lightly spray a cookie sheet with cooking spray.

3. Combine the poppy seeds, onion and garlic powders, and salt in a small mixing bowl.

4. Roll out the crescent dough and separate it into the 8 prepared sections. Spread Dijon mustard on each section of dough.

5. Then, roll the hotdogs up in the rolls, starting with the hotdog at the skinny end of the roll.

6. Brush the rolls with egg and sprinkle the poppy seed seasoning mix across each dog roll.

7. Place the rolls on the cookie sheet and place it on the grill.

8. Cover the grill and cook for 20 to 25 minutes, or until the rolls are golden brown.

9. Remove from heat, let stand 2 to 3 minutes, and serve.

FULLY LOADED JUICY WIENERS

Trust me, these fully loaded dogs are the juiciest and plumpest wieners you'll ever taste. With a variety of toppings, each dog can be personalized to your desired porker preferences.

GRILL: ANY GRILL | PREP TIME: 10 TO 12 MINUTES | COOK TIME: 11 TO 14 MINUTES | MAKES: 8 SERVINGS

HOT DOGS

8 hot dogs

olive or vegetable oil

8 hot dog buns

½ bell pepper, thinly sliced

¼ red onion, thinly sliced

½ stick melted garlic butter

TOPPINGS

horseradish sauce

ketchup

pickle relish

mustard

sauerkraut

shredded cheddar cheese

sliced or chopped onions

INSTRUCTIONS

1. Preheat the grill to 425°F.

2. Make 4 to 5 small slits in each hot dog.

3. On a rimmed baking sheet, lay out one layer of heavy-duty aluminum foil.

4. Lightly spray the foil with olive or vegetable cooking oil.

5. Place the sliced veggies on the foil and immediately put the baking sheet on the grill. Cook until the veggies are tender, about 7-10 minutes.

6. Carefully place each hot dog on the grill and cook for 2 to 3 minutes.

7. Rotate the hot dogs with tongs and cook for another 2 to 3 minutes.

8. While the hot dogs are cooking, butter your hotdog buns with garlic butter.

9. Rotate the hot dogs one last time and cook for another 2 to 3 minutes.

10. About 2 minutes before you remove the hot dogs from the grill, place the hot dog buns on the grill, butter side down. Heat for 1 minute.

11. Remove the hot dogs and immediately put them into buns.

12. Remove the grilled veggies and let them stand for 1 to 2 minutes before adding them to the hot dogs.

13. Add any combination of topping suggestions, and enjoy!

TASTES
LIKE COCK

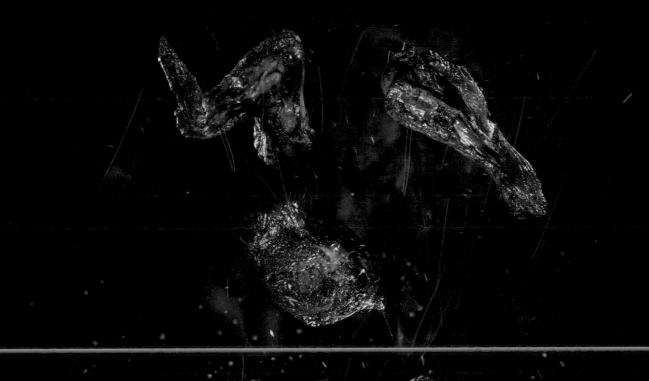

BOW-CHICK-A-WOW-WOW DRUMSTICKS

Bone in. Skin on. These legs are about to rock your world. With minimal prep and an easy grilling method, I predict this will become your go-to move. And fair warning, after you enjoy all this cock, you're going to need extra napkins to clean up your messy hands and mouth.

**GRILL: ANY GRILL | PREP TIME: 10 MINUTES |
COOK TIME: 15 TO 20 MINUTES | MAKES: 3 TO 4 SERVINGS**

6 to 8 chicken legs

2 tablespoons garlic powder

1 tablespoon onion powder

1 tablespoon sugar

1 teaspoon paprika

2 teaspoons chili powder

¼ teaspoon ground cinnamon

½ teaspoon cayenne pepper

½ teaspoon ground mustard

½ teaspoon salt

1 teaspoon ground black pepper

½ teaspoon ground cumin

¼ cup vegetable or olive oil

INSTRUCTIONS

1. Preheat the grill to 425°F.

2. Rinse the chicken legs and pat them dry with paper towels. Set aside.

3. Combine the seasonings and sugar in a jar or bottle and shake thoroughly until well incorporated.

4. Brush the oil on all sides of each chicken leg, then dump some of the dry rub mix onto them. Massage the rub into the skin until the sexy legs are thoroughly coated with the rub.

5. Brush oil on the grill grate and put the chicken on the grate over the open flames.

6. Cook for 15 to 20 minutes, rotating the legs every 5 minutes.

7. Use a thermometer to check the internal temperature. When it reaches 165°F, the cock is done.

8. Remove the chicken from the grill and let it stand for 5 minutes before serving.

CREAMY ITALIAN THIGHS (TUSCAN CHICKEN)

Simple, comforting, delicious, and it doesn't disappoint—how else would you describe this Italian cock? It's rich, tasty, and oh-so-creamy. To round out the meal, you can serve this over any sort of bed—rice, pasta, or couscous.

**GRILL: GAS GRILL IDEALLY | PREP TIME: 12 TO 15 MINUTES |
COOK TIME: 10 TO 13 MINUTES | MAKES: 4 SERVINGS**

1½ cups heavy cream

3 tablespoons butter, melted

1 tablespoon olive oil

½ tablespoon dried oregano

¼ teaspoon salt

½ teaspoon ground black pepper

1 teaspoon dried minced onion

½ teaspoon dried rosemary

½ teaspoon dried thyme

¼ cup grated Parmesan cheese

4 cloves garlic, minced

4 boneless, skinless chicken thighs

½ cup sun-dried tomatoes (optional)

½ cup olives (optional)

fresh dill, cilantro, or basil, for garnish

INSTRUCTIONS

1. In a medium mixing bowl, whisk the heavy cream, butter, oil, and the six seasonings.

2. When it is thoroughly incorporated, add the Parmesan, garlic, cilantro, and basil. Whisk until thoroughly blended and the herb leaves are coated.

3. Preheat the grill to medium-high.

4. Spray a cast-iron skillet with olive oil cooking spray and place it on the grill. Preheat for 5 minutes.

5. When the pan is ready, pour in about half of the cream mixture. Add the chicken thighs and let them cook for 2 to 3 minutes.

6. Add the remainder of the cream mixture and cook the chicken for 3 to 5 minutes, spooning the cream sauce over the chicken regularly.

7. Flip the chicken and continue spooning the sauce over the meat.

8. Add the sun-dried tomatoes and olives, if using.

9. Let the cock cook for another 3 to 5 minutes, or until the meat reaches an internal temperature of 165°F.

10. When the chicken has finished cooking, remove it from the grill and let it cool for 5 minutes before plating.

11. Garnish with additional basil or cilantro leaves. Serve and enjoy.

SPREAD-EM-AND-RUB-EM SPATCHCOCK CHICKEN

If the chicken is a-spatchcockin', don't come a-knockin'! I think we can all agree we love shortcuts that save time yet still produce a food-gasmic end result. Enter the slutty chicken that's spreading herself wide open for your culinary pleasure. This butterflied chicken will cook in half the time of a whole cock—and it cooks more evenly, too. You might be nervous your first time spatchcocking, but you'll never look back once you try it.

GRILL: ANY GRILL | PREP TIME: 10 TO 15 MINUTES | COOK TIME: 50 MINUTES | MAKES: 8 TO 10 SERVINGS

1 (5-pound) chicken

2 tablespoons brown sugar, packed

1 teaspoon salt

1 teaspoon paprika

1 tablespoon garlic powder

1 tablespoon onion powder

1 teaspoon ground black pepper

1 tablespoon dried oregano

2 teaspoons paprika

½ teaspoon ground cumin

½ teaspoon ground coriander

½ teaspoon ground mustard

½ teaspoon celery seed

INSTRUCTIONS

1. Remove and dispose of any organs inside the chicken.

2. Rinse the bird and pat it dry with paper towels.

3. Next, place the bird on a large cutting board, breast down, inner cavity facing toward you.

4. Using heavy-duty kitchen shears, cut a straight line up the right side of the backbone, from the tail to the neck. (You may need to double-hand the scissors for enough leverage.)

5. Repeat on the left side of the bird.

6. Remove the backbone of the bird and discard it or use it for chicken stock, as desired.

7. Next, break the breastbone by flipping the bird over, breast side up. Separate the back and press down on the breast with the heel of your hand until the bird is lying flat on the cutting board.

8. Tuck the tips of the wings behind the shoulders of the bird to prevent them from burning.

9. Turn out the legs so that they are even. Set the chicken aside.

10. Preheat the grill to medium-high and cover it.

11. Combine the sugar and the 11 spices in a jar or bottle and shake it until completely incorporated.

12. Brush the bird with olive oil.

13. Rub the sugar and spice mix onto the skin of the chicken.

14. Place the chicken on the grill and cook for 15 minutes.

15. Flip the chick over and cook for another 30 minutes.

16. Flip the bird again and check to see if the internal temperature has reached 165°F. Flip it again and cook for 5 more minutes.

17. Remove it from grill and let it stand for 10 minutes before carving and serving.

No one will leave without getting theirs at this cock-a-doodle-doo rodeo. Though it's a quickie—you will not need more than 30 minutes total—the memory of how hot and spicy it was will linger with you for days after the rendezvous.

**GRILL: GAS OR CHARCOAL | PREP TIME: 7 TO 10 MINUTES |
COOK TIME: 15 MINUTES + 10 MINUTES | MAKES: 4 LARGE FAJITAS**

SPICE RUB

4 teaspoons chili powder

2 teaspoons paprika

1 teaspoon onion powder

1 teaspoon garlic powder

½ teaspoon cayenne pepper

½ teaspoon ground cumin

FAJITA SAUCE

juice of 1 lime

juice of 1 lemon

2 cloves garlic, minced

1 tablespoon ground cumin

½ teaspoon paprika

1 tablespoon olive oil

1 teaspoon honey

FAJITAS

1 large boneless, skinless chicken breast

cooking spray

2 red peppers, sliced

1 red onion, sliced

4 large flour tortillas

INSTRUCTIONS

1. Preheat the grill to 350°F.

2. To make the spice rub, combine all the ingredients in a jar and shake thoroughly until fully incorporated.

3. Rinse the chicken breast and pat it dry with a paper towel.

4. Lightly spray the chicken breast on all sides with cooking spray.

5. Gently massage the spice rub onto the chicken on all sides and place it on the grill. Cook for 7 to 8 minutes.

6. Flip the bird and finish cooking it on other side, another 7 to 8 minutes.

7. While the chicken is grilling, lightly spray a cast-iron skillet with cooking spray and preheat it on the grill for 2 to 3 minutes.

8. Add the vegetables with the remainder of the spice rub to the skillet.

9. Stir the ingredients to coat the veggies with the rub.

10. Let the veggies cook, stirring occasionally, until they start to soften, 7 to 10 minutes.

11. Remove the skillet from the heat and set it aside.

12. When the chicken has finished cooking, remove it from the grill and use a fork to shred the meat, including the charred chicken.

13. Add the meat to the veggies and set it aside.

14. Combine the ingredients for fajita sauce in an air-tight jar and shake it vigorously until ingredients are thoroughly combined.

15. Place the tortillas on a plate and microwave for 30 seconds to warm slightly.

16. Plate the tortillas, filling them with the chicken and vegetable mix, and drizzled with the fajita sauce. Serve immediately.

Inspired by a dish I had in New Orleans, this is the best cock I've ever had in my life. It took some trial and error, but I was finally able to duplicate this sexy bird at home. If you're into legs, these sticky, sweet, succulent thighs will satisfy all your cravings.

GRILL: ANY GRILL | PREP TIME: 5 TO 7 MINUTES | CHILL TIME: 4 TO 8 HOURS | COOK TIME: 14 TO 20 MINUTES | MAKES: 8 SERVINGS

8 boneless, skinless chicken thighs

⅓ cup teriyaki sauce

¼ cup light brown sugar, packed

2 tablespoons honey

1 tablespoon olive oil

1 tablespoon apple cider vinegar

4 cloves garlic, minced

1 teaspoon dried basil

2 teaspoons dried oregano

1 teaspoon smoked paprika

½ teaspoon ground black pepper

¼ teaspoon salt

1 teaspoon cayenne pepper

½ teaspoon ground ginger

INSTRUCTIONS

1. In a small mixing bowl, whisk the teriyaki sauce, brown sugar, honey, oil, vinegar, garlic and the 7 seasonings until thoroughly incorporated.

2. Reserve one-third of the marinade for use later. Pour the remainder into a ziplock bag.

3. Add the thighs to the bag and massage the marinade into the meat, until all of it is coated.

4. Let the chicken marinate in the refrigerator for 4 to 8 hours.

5. When you're ready to cook, remove the bird from the refrigerator and let it stand for 15 minutes. Prepare the grill in the meantime.

6. Preheat the grill to medium-high.

7. When the chicken has been standing for 15 minutes, brush some oil onto the grate of the grill.

8. Place the chicken on the grill and discard the leftover marinade.

9. Cook over direct heat for 5 to 8 minutes.

10. Flip the meat and cook for another 5 to 8 minutes, until internal temperature reaches 165°F.

11. Use the reserved marinade to baste the chicken. Cook for 2 minutes.

12. Flip the chicken, baste it again, and cook for another 2 minutes.

13. Remove the thighs from the grill and let them stand for 5 minutes before serving.

SEASONED DARK MEAT WITH WHITE CREAM SAUCE

Dark meat, a delicious buttery creamy sauce—this cock is serving up something for everyone. And it makes for great leftovers when you just aren't in the mood… to cook.

GRILL: ANY GRILL | PREP TIME: 3 TO 5 MINUTES |
COOK TIME: 10 TO 12 MINUTES + 14 TO 17 MINUTES | MAKES: 4 SERVINGS

CHICKEN

1 tablespoon sugar

1 tablespoon paprika

1 teaspoon garlic powder

1 teaspoon onion powder

½ teaspoon salt

½ teaspoon ground black pepper

½ teaspoon ground coriander

CREAM SAUCE

1 tablespoon butter

1 tablespoon olive oil

6 cloves garlic, minced

1 tablespoon all-purpose flour

1 cup heavy cream

4 boneless chicken thighs

olive oil

fresh dill, for garnish

½ cup chicken broth

1 cup sliced white mushrooms

½ cup grated Parmesan cheese

4 ounces cream cheese

TO MAKE THE CHICKEN

1. Preheat the grill to medium-high.

2. Combine the sugar and the six seasonings in a jar or bottle and shake thoroughly.

3. Rinse the chicken thighs and pat them dry with paper towels.

4. Lightly brush the chicken with olive oil and then massage the rub into the meat.

5. Next, lightly brush the grill grate with olive oil.

6. Place the chicken on the grill, away from the fire, and cook it for 5 to 6 minutes on each side.

7. Use a thermometer to check the internal temperature. At 165°F, the chicken is done.

8. Remove it from the grill and let it stand for 5 minutes before serving with the cream sauce.

TO MAKE THE CREAM SAUCE

1. In a medium saucepan, melt the butter and oil over medium heat, 2 to 3 minutes.

2. Add the garlic and cook, stirring, for 2 minutes.

3. Add the flour and stir while cooking for 2 minutes.

4. Next, add the heavy cream and broth and stir until the sauce thickens, 3 to 5 minutes.

5. Now add the mushrooms, Parmesan, and cream cheese. Stir constantly as you continue cooking for 5 minutes.

6. Remove the sauce from the heat and spoon it over the chicken. Garnish with fresh dill, as desired. Serve immediately.

TENDER, THAI-MASSAGED BREASTS

The secret to these tender breasts absorbing all the tasty juices is the intimate swim they take while cooking. It gets hot and steamy!

**GRILL: GAS GRILL IDEALLY | PREP TIME: 10 MINUTES |
COOK TIME: 16 TO 23 MINUTES + 5 TO 7 MINUTES | MAKES: 4 SERVINGS**

CHICKEN

juice of 2 limes

2 tablespoons sesame oil

2 tablespoons honey

¼ cup teriyaki sauce

1 tablespoon sesame seeds

3 tablespoons brown sugar, packed

¼ teaspoon chili powder

1 teaspoon ground black pepper

1 tablespoon yellow or red curry powder

1 teaspoon ground ginger

4 boneless, skinless chicken breasts

2 green onions, thinly sliced

6 cloves garlic, minced

1 large handful of fresh cilantro leaves

fresh cilantro or basil, for garnish (optional)

PEANUT SAUCE

1 (13.5-ounce) can coconut milk

¼ cup smooth peanut butter

¼ cup brown sugar, packed

1 tablespoon teriyaki sauce

1 teaspoon yellow or red curry powder

3 tablespoons all-purpose flour

TO MAKE THE CHICKEN

1. Preheat the grill to 425°F.

2. In a medium bowl, combine the lime juice, sesame oil, honey, teriyaki sauce, sesame seeds, and the sugar and the 4 seasonings. Stir until well incorporated.

3. Pour the oil mixture into a cast-iron skillet and place it on the grill over direct heat. Heat it for 3 to 5 minutes.

4. Add the chicken breasts and, using a ladle, cover the meat with the oil mixture.

5. Cook for 7 to 10 minutes or until the meat begins to look slightly dark and charred.

6. Flip the meat and baste it again, using the ladle.

7. Cook for another 7 to 10 minutes, then add the green onions, garlic and fresh cilantro leaves.

8. Stir the sauce and herbs for 2 to 3 minutes, ladling over the chicken regularly.

9. Use a meat thermometer to check the internal temperature of the chicken. If the meat has reached 165°F, it is done and you may remove it from the grill. If not, let it cook for another 3 to 5 minutes and test the temperature again.

10. When the chicken has been removed from the grill, let it stand for 3 to 5 minutes before serving with a healthy covering of the peanut sauce.

TO MAKE THE PEANUT SAUCE

1. On the stovetop, combine all the ingredients, in order, in a saucepan over medium-high heat.

2. Whisking constantly, cooking for 3 to 5 minutes until the sauce begins to bubble.

3. Reduce the heat to medium and continue whisking until the tangy sauce is smooth and thick, about 2 minutes.

4. Remove the sauce from the heat and let it stand 5 minutes before serving.

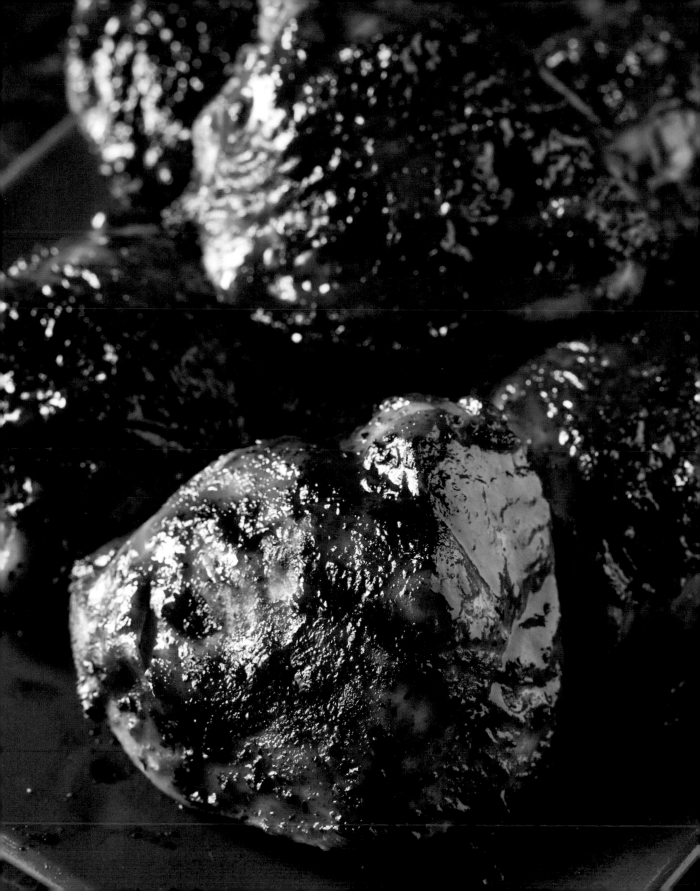

Share your beer with this bird and you'll discover tender, moist, falling-off-the-bone meat with a crispy, tangy skin. It's the best of both worlds.

**GRILL: ANY GRILL | PREP TIME: 7 TO 10 MINUTES |
CHILL TIME: OVERNIGHT | COOK TIME: 25 MINUTES | MAKES: 4 SERVINGS**

½ cup olive oil

1 teaspoon salt

½ teaspoon ground black pepper

½ teaspoon ground cumin

1 teaspoon yellow curry powder

¼ teaspoon cayenne pepper

2 tablespoons honey

4 cloves garlic, minced

1 red onion

1 red bell pepper

1⅓ cups of your favorite dark beer

4 chicken breasts or 8 drumsticks/thighs

INSTRUCTIONS

1. Pour the olive oil into a large mixing bowl.

2. In a small mixing bowl, whisk the five seasonings together.

3. Add the seasonings to the large bowl.

4. Add the honey, garlic, onions, and bell pepper. Mix with a fork.

5. Now add the beer slowly, allowing it to foam and bubble. Mix until everything is thoroughly incorporated.

6. Put the chicken in a ziplock bag then add the marinade.

7. Seal the bag and massage the brewed mix into the chicken. Release the air in the bag, fold the bag in half, and refrigerate overnight.

8. When you're ready to cook, preheat the grill to 350°F. Place the chicken on the grill and dispose of the marinade.

9. Turn the chicken every 5 minutes, cooking it for 25 minutes total or until the internal temperature reaches 165°F.

10. Remove the chicken from the grill and serve immediately.

BOUND CHICKEN STICKS (PROSCIUTTO-WRAPPED CHICKEN KEBABS)

What makes this recipe promiscuous? The two types of meat coming together in one tantalizingly savory and seductive bite. Pop a couple of cherry tomatoes for an intensified food-gasm.

GRILL: GAS OR CHARCOAL | PREP TIME: 25 MINUTES | CHILL TIME: 4 TO 8 HOURS | COOK TIME: 14 TO 18 MINUTES | MAKES: 15 TO 18 SKEWERS

MARINADE

juice of 1 lime

¼ cup olive oil

1 tablespoon apple cider vinegar

handful of fresh cilantro

½ teaspoon dried rosemary

½ teaspoon dried thyme

½ teaspoon garlic powder

1 teaspoon onion powder

KEBABS

2 pounds boneless, skinless chicken breast, cut into 2-inch cubes

8 ounces prosciutto

2 sweet red bell peppers, cut into chunks

30 to 36 cherry tomatoes

INSTRUCTIONS

1. Combine all the ingredients for the marinade in a ziplock bag.

2. Add the cubes of tender breast meat.

3. Massage the marinade and chicken together until the cock is thoroughly coated on all sides.

4. Press the air out of the bag, seal the bag, and refrigerate it for 4 to 8 hours.

5. Preheat the grill to 350°F.

6. While the grill is heating up, remove the cock from the marinade and set on a plate or cutting board.

7. Cut the savory prosciutto slices in half, lengthwise.

8. As if it's a special meat-on-meat present, wrap each chunk of chicken with a piece of prosciutto.

9. Pierce two chunks of prosciutto-wrapped chicken on each bamboo or metal skewer, alternating them with cherry tomatoes and sweet red pepper.

10. Place the promiscuous skewers on the grill and cook for 7 to 8 minutes.

11. Flip the seductive skewers and cook on the other side for another 7 to 8 minutes.

12. Serve immediately.

SUCH-A-TEASE PRUDISH HENS (CORNISH HENS)

These hens want to be big and bad like their cocky relatives. Yet they can't change who they are at their core. When you're looking to impress guests or relatives, turn to the prudish hens for a simple, elegant meal that never fails.

GRILL: CHARCOAL GRILL OR SMOKER | PREP TIME: 15 MINUTES | COOK TIME: 1 HOUR | MAKES: 6 SERVINGS

2 cups cherry wood chips for smoking

2 cups apple wood chips for smoking

6 Cornish hens

olive oil

2 tablespoons apple cider vinegar

1 cup apple juice

juice of 1 lemon

1 cup brown sugar, packed

2 tablespoons honey

1 tablespoon garlic powder

1 teaspoon ground ginger

1 large red onion, chopped

4 green onions, chopped

2 cups strawberries, fresh or frozen

2 cups blueberries, fresh or frozen

leaves from 1 sprig fresh rosemary

INSTRUCTIONS

1. Preheat the grill to medium-high, using the wood chips to add smoke. Leave the grate off.

2. Lay out six double layers of aluminum foil, folding the edges up into bowls for the hens.

3. Rinse the Cornish hens and pat dry with paper towels.

4. Place each hen into one of the foil packets. Brush each hen with olive oil.

5. In a small mixing bowl, combine the vinegar, apple juice, lemon juice, sugar, honey, and garlic and ginger powders. Whisk together until thoroughly combined.

6. Evenly distribute the onions, berries, and fresh rosemary in the 6 foil packets.

7. Pour the juice mixture into the packets, then seal the packets tightly.

8. Place the packets directly into the charcoal of the fire. Cover the grill.

9. Cook for 1 hour, then check the internal temperature. The internal temp should read 180°F.

10. Remove the foil packets from the grill and let them stand for 5 minutes. Peel back the top of the foil and let stand another 5 minutes.

11. Plate the hens, spooning the berries, onions, and sauce over them.

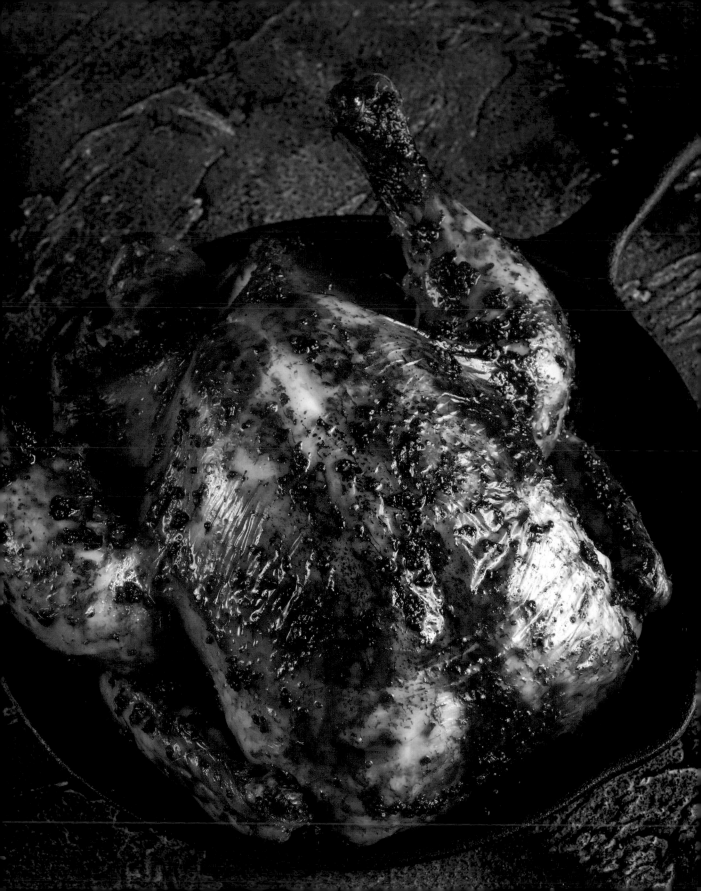

You're on a date. You really like this person, but you haven't slept together yet. You're thinking tonight could be the night. The cock expectations could really be anywhere on the spectrum. Big or small? Thick or thin? There are just so many questions. The only way to get the answers is to see the cock for yourself. Now imagine it's the biggest, most beautiful dick you've ever seen in your entire life. And this ana-cock-a knows exactly what to do to pleasure you. Well, this is that—but as a stunning, roasted chicken served on a silver platter.

**GRILL: CHARCOAL GRILL OR SMOKER | PREP TIME: 10 MINUTES |
CHILL TIME: OVERNIGHT | COOK TIME: 1³/₄ HOURS | MAKES: 4 TO 6 SERVINGS**

6 cups cold water

½ cup salt

1 (4 to 4½-pound) chicken

3 tablespoons olive oil

juice and zest of 1 lime

juice and zest of 1 lemon

1 white onion, thinly sliced

1 teaspoon garlic powder

1 teaspoon onion powder

1 teaspoon dried rosemary

1 teaspoon dried thyme

1 teaspoon ground coriander

INSTRUCTIONS

1. Whisk together the water and salt in a bowl large enough to hold the chicken.

2. Place the chicken in the salted water. Cover and refrigerate it overnight.

3. Preheat the grill to medium-low.

4. Remove the chicken from the brine. Rinse it, then pat it dry with paper towels.

5. Combine the remaining ingredients in a medium mixing bowl.

6. Brush the oil and juice mixture over the chicken, stuffing the onion slices into the cavity of the chicken.

7. Place the chicken on the grill, away from the direct heat.

8. Cook the chicken for 7 minutes, then turn it over and cook it for another 7 minutes. Char marks should be visible.

9. Cover the grill and cook for another 1½ hours.

10. Check the internal temperature where the thighs meet the rest of the body, avoiding any bones. When the temperature reaches 165°F, remove the bird from the grill.

11. Let it stand for 10 minutes before carving.

It's time to pound out your cock. These thighs are going to take a beating. Just the (Pro) Tip: Go light on the pepper if you can't handle intense heat and spice. And make sure to thoroughly wash your hands after handling the hot pepper—we don't want any accidental burns.

GRILL: ANY GRILL | PREP TIME: 10 MINUTES | CHILL TIME: 4 TO 8 HOURS | COOK TIME: 35 MINUTES | MAKES: 4 TO 6 SERVINGS

1 yellow onion, cut into large chunks

3 green onions, quartered

1 hot pepper (Habanero, Scotch bonnet, or jalapeño), to taste

4 cloves garlic, minced

¼ cup fresh lime juice

¼ cup soy sauce

2 tablespoons olive oil

2 tablespoons brown sugar, packed

½ teaspoon ground allspice

½ teaspoon dried thyme

½ teaspoon ground nutmeg

1 teaspoon salt

2 teaspoons ground black pepper

4 to 4½ pounds chicken thighs and drumsticks

INSTRUCTIONS

1. Combine all the ingredients, except the chicken, in the bowl of a food processor.

2. Pour the marinade into a ziplock bag, along with the chicken, and seal the bag.

3. Massage the marinade into the chicken, then place the bag in the refrigerator. Chill for 4 to 8 hours.

4. Remove the chicken and let it return to room temperature before grilling.

5. Preheat the grill to medium-high.

6. Brush the grate with olive oil.

7. Place the chicken on the grill, skin side down, cover the grill, and cook for 10 minutes.

8. Flip the chicken over, cover it again, and cook for another 10 minutes.

9. Move the chicken to a cooler section of the grill and cook for another 15 minutes, covered.

10. Remove it from the grill and serve immediately.

TENDERIZED, DRIPPING-WET COCK (BUTTERMILK CHICKEN)

Buttermilk is most often associated with fried cock, but here, it tenderizes the meat and helps to highlight the garlic and chili and cumin seasonings. This cock is drowning in creamy juices, just the way I like it.

GRILL: ANY GRILL | PREP TIME: 5 TO 7 MINUTES |
COOK TIME: 20 MINUTES | MAKES: 6 SERVINGS

2 cups buttermilk

1 lime, zested and juiced

2 tablespoons olive oil

4 cloves garlic, minced

1 tablespoon chili powder

1 tablespoon ground cumin

2 teaspoons coarsely chopped fresh cilantro, for garnish

fresh whole basil leaves, for garnish

pinch of ground black pepper

pinch of salt

4 pounds boneless, skinless chicken breasts

INSTRUCTIONS

1. Preheat the grill to medium-high.

2. Lightly oil a large cast-iron skillet with olive oil. Place it on the grill to preheat.

3. In a medium mixing bowl, combine all the ingredients except the chicken and whisk together.

4. Pour a small amount of the buttermilk mixture into the preheated pan.

5. Add the chicken breasts and pour the rest of the buttermilk mixture over the chicken.

6. Cook for 20 minutes, using tongs to flip the chicken every few minutes. Continually stir the sauce and ladle it over the chicken.

7. When the internal temperature reaches 165°F, remove the chicken from the grill.

8. Let it stand for 5 minutes, garnish with chopped cilantro and basil leaves, and serve.

A bit of butter goes a long way in making these breasts both scrumptious and as juicy as can be. One little nipple—er, I mean nibble—and you'll immediately have a new favorite way to fondle and serve your breasts.

**GRILL: ANY GRILL | PREP TIME: 5 MINUTES |
COOK TIME: 20 MINUTES | MAKES: 4 SERVINGS**

⅓ cup butter, melted

1 teaspoon paprika

½ teaspoon salt

½ teaspoon ground black pepper

1 teaspoon onion powder

2 teaspoon garlic powder

1 teaspoon sugar

8 skinless bone-in chicken breasts

INSTRUCTIONS

1. Preheat the grill to medium-high.

2. Place a cast-iron skillet on the grill to preheat.

3. In a mixing bowl, combine all the ingredients except the chicken, and whisk together.

4. Spoon a couple tablespoons of the butter mixture into the pan. Roll the pan to coat the bottom of the pan.

5. Place the chicken in the pan and gently pour the rest of the butter sauce over the chicken.

6. Cook for 20 minutes, using tongs to flip the chicken every few minutes. Continually stir the sauce and ladle over the chicken.

7. When the internal temperature reaches 165°F, remove the pan from the grill.

8. Let stand for 5 minutes, then serve.

Move over, Engagement Chicken. This cock will have an aphrodisiac effect on you, inspiring you to go all night long as well. These breasts are best served after having a passionate night bathing in the tangy marinade. When you've placed the breasts in the cool fridge, don't disturb the meat. Allow it to have a little privacy overnight as the breasts absorb the sweet and savory juices. Trust me, this cock does not disappoint.

GRILL: GAS OR CHARCOAL | PREP TIME: 5 MINUTES | CHILL TIME: OVERNIGHT | COOK TIME: 15 TO 20 MINUTES | MAKES: 4 SERVINGS

4 boneless, skinless chicken breasts

2 tablespoons olive oil

juice of 2 oranges

¼ cup honey

1½ teaspoons onion powder

½ teaspoon garlic powder

¼ teaspoon cayenne pepper

¼ teaspoon ground black pepper

¼ teaspoon ground sea salt

¾ teaspoon ground cinnamon

INSTRUCTIONS

1. Rinse the breasts, then gently fondle and pat them dry with a paper towel.

2. Cut several slits into each chicken breast, then place in a ziplock bag.

3. Whisk the remaining ingredients and add the mixture to the bag with chicken, then passionately massage them together until the chicken is completely coated in the savory juices.

4. Press the air out of the bag, seal it, and refrigerate it overnight.

5. Preheat the grill to high.

6. When grill has reached full temperature, place your marinated cock on the grill and cook it for 7 to 10 minutes.

7. Flip the bird and cook it for another 7 to 10 minutes.

8. Serve immediately.

STEAMY, SLIPPERY SEAFOOD

DOWN-'N'-DIRTY SHRIMP

JUST THE (PRO) TIP: Increase the heat by upping the amount of crushed red pepper or chili powder you use. Serve the shrimp on its own, or on a sexy bed of buttered pasta or a seductive, crunchy salad.

GRILL: GAS OR CHARCOAL | PREP TIME: 7 MINUTES | CHILL TIME: 4 TO 8 HOURS | COOK TIME: 4 TO 6 MINUTES | MAKES: 6 TO 8 SKEWERS

3/4 pound shrimp, peeled

juice of 2 limes

juice of 1 lemon

juice of 1 blood orange

3 cloves garlic, pressed

1 teaspoon dried minced onion

1½ teaspoons ground cumin

1 teaspoon crushed red pepper

1 teaspoon chili powder

INSTRUCTIONS

1. Whisk all the ingredients except the shrimp and add the mixture with the shrimp to a ziplock bag. Shake it up, down, and side-to-side to thoroughly coat the shrimp.

2. Seal the container and chill it for 4 to 8 hours.

3. When the shrimp has absorbed the juices, preheat the grill to 450°F.

4. Remove the shrimp from the marinade and seductively slide it onto bamboo or steel skewers and place them on the grill.

5. Cook the shrimp for 2 to 3 minutes until perfectly pink.

6. Flip the skewers and cook for another 2 to 3 minutes.

7. Serve immediately.

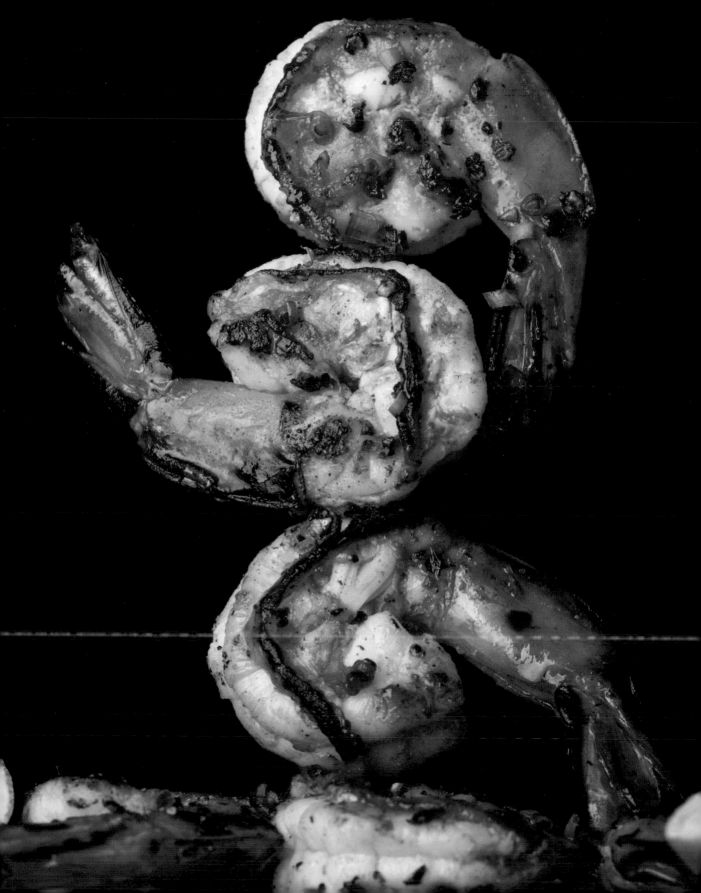

Perfect for a larger summer gathering, this dish can be cooked on the grill or on the stovetop. The secret to a mouthwatering clambake is layering the ingredients to let the flavors be single and mingle with one another. It's a one-pot meal with clams, shrimp, corn, potatoes, and whatever else you'd like to throw in. It's like a delicious, magical orgy for your taste buds.

GRILL: ANY GRILL | PREP TIME: 15 MINUTES | COOK TIME: 1 HOUR | MAKES: 10 TO 12 SERVINGS

2 cups white wine

1 cup butter, melted

6 cloves garlic, minced

⅓ cup fresh basil, chopped

⅓ cup fresh dill, chopped

¼ cup fresh chives, chopped

6 sprigs fresh thyme

2 tablespoons salt

½ tablespoon ground black pepper

1 tablespoon sugar

½ cup olive oil

2 teaspoons smoked paprika

1 tablespoon dried oregano

2 pounds large tail-on raw shrimp, deveined

4 ears of corn, cut into quarters

2 pounds baby red potatoes, cut in half

4 dozen littleneck clams

2 large onions, cut into eighths

1½ pounds precooked sausage, cut into bite-sized pieces

2 cups cherry tomatoes, sliced in half

several lemons, quartered, for service

fresh curly parsley, for garnish (optional)

INSTRUCTIONS

1. Preheat the grill to medium-high.

2. Combine the wine, butter, garlic, basil, dill, chives, thyme, salt, pepper, sugar, olive oil, paprika, and oregano in a medium mixing bowl. Whisk until well blended.

3. In a large stockpot, combine the shrimp, corn, potatoes, clams, onions, sausage, and tomatoes.

4. Pour the wine sauce mixture into the stockpot. With a long-handled spoon (*wink*), stir the ingredients together over the meaty materials and vegetables.

5. Cook for 45 minutes to 1 hour, until the clams open, the potatoes are tender, and the shrimp turn pink, stirring regularly, spooning the savory fluids over the other ingredients.

6. When the meal is cooked, remove the stockpot from the grill and let it stand for 10 minutes before serving.

7. Serve with lemon wedges and garnish with fresh parsley, if desired.

PERFECTLY PINK AND JUICY SALMON TACOS

The recipe name says it all. This dish is not only easy to make, but the juicy salmon tacos are also incredibly light, fresh, and oh-so-satisfying. One taste of this pink taco and you'll be craving taco takeout for days and nights to cum.

GRILL: CHARCOAL | PREP TIME: 15 MINUTES | COOK TIME: 7 TO 11 MINUTES | MAKES: 4 TO 6 TACOS

SALMON

½ tablespoon chili powder

1 tablespoon ground cumin

½ teaspoon sea salt

1 teaspoon ground black pepper

1 tablespoon garlic powder

½ tablespoon onion powder

½ teaspoon crushed red pepper

2 teaspoons paprika

1 teaspoon cayenne pepper

1 pound fresh salmon

olive oil cooking spray

TACOS

juice of 1 lemon

juice of 1 lime

1 yellow or orange bell pepper, diced

2 Roma tomatoes, diced

1 cup fresh spinach, chopped

½ large red onion, diced

4 to 6 taco-size flour tortillas

salsa (optional)

INSTRUCTIONS

1. Preheat the grill to 450°F, placing charcoal on one side for direct high heat and the other side for indirect heat.

2. Combine the 9 ingredients for the rub in a jar and shake it thoroughly until well blended. Set it aside.

3. Rinse the salmon and pat it dry with a paper towel.

4. Lightly coat the salmon with olive oil cooking spray.

5. Gently massage the spice rub into all sides of the salmon.

6. When the grill is hot, brush the grill grate with oil. (Dip a paper towel in olive oil and use tongs to rub it across the grate.)

7. Gently place the salmon on the grill, skin side up.

8. Cook it for 3 to 4 minutes, until grill marks appear.

9. Using tongs and a spatula, if needed, gently turn the salmon over and cook it for another 4 to 7 minutes. Remove it from the heat and set it aside.

10. In a ziplock bag, combine the lemon and lime juices and the chopped vegetables. Shake thoroughly until the veggies are coated with the juice.

11. Shred the salmon meat into tortillas and top with the wet mixed vegetables.

12. Top with salsa, if desired, and serve immediately.

SHUCK-ME-GOOD GRILLED OYSTERS

Yes, we all know oysters are an aphrodisiac. And we also know oysters are a great appetizer to order for the table. But why risk getting all turned on and hot and bothered when you're dining at a restaurant? Bring the romance and passion home by grilling oysters together with your date. It's as easy as 1-2-3: Grill, slurp, and go shuck.

GRILL: ANY GRILL | PREP TIME: 5 MINUTES |
COOK TIME: 7 MINUTES | MAKES: 10 TO 12 SERVINGS

1 cup butter, softened

¼ cup finely chopped fresh parsley

3 cloves garlic, minced

1 teaspoon Worcestershire sauce

1 teaspoon paprika

½ teaspoon ground red pepper

¼ teaspoon ground black pepper

½ teaspoon hot sauce of choice

1 teaspoon lemon juice

2 dozen fresh oysters on the half shell

lemon wedges, for service

INSTRUCTIONS

1. Preheat the grill to 450°F.

2. In a food processor or blender, pulse together all the ingredients except the oysters and lemon wedges, until thoroughly combined.

3. Arrange the oysters in a single layer on the grill.

4. Spoon 2 teaspoons of the butter mixture into each oyster.

5. Grill the oysters, uncovered, for 7 minutes, or until the edges of the meat begin to curl.

6. Remove them from the grill and serve immediately with the lemon wedges.

SMOKING-HOT MUSSELS

In French, this recipe is called "Moules fumées à chaud." It truly is a specialty—the recipe has been passed down through the generations of my family, dating as far back as my great-grandmother's great-grandmother. The story goes that she was so enamored with the owner of a local smoke-shop in her old French village. Great-granny was so mesmerized by Henri's muscles that she knew the only way to get his attention was through her mussels. It's rumored that she got knocked up that night. And if she hadn't shown off her guns in the kitchen, I wouldn't be here writing this cookbook today. *Merci, Grand-mère!*

JUST THE (PRO) TIP: This recipe calls for white wine. Make sure to pour yourself a glass or two to enjoy while you cook as well!

GRILL: CHARCOAL GRILL OR SMOKER | PREP TIME: 20 MINUTES |
CHILL TIME: 2 HOURS | COOK TIME: 8 TO 10 MINUTES | MAKES: 4 SERVINGS

ORANGE SAFFRON AIOLI SAUCE

1 large orange

pinch of saffron, crumbled threads

3 cloves garlic, minced

1½ teaspoons Dijon mustard

1 large egg yolk

½ cup olive oil

½ cup vegetable oil

pinch of salt

¼ cup pitted and finely chopped Niçoise olives

MUSSELS

2 pounds mussels

3 tablespoons butter, melted

2 tablespoons dry white wine

1 lime, zested and juiced

1 tablespoon olive oil

⅛ teaspoon salt

⅛ teaspoon ground black pepper

½ teaspoon ground cumin

¼ teaspoon crushed red pepper

2 tablespoons fresh parsley, chopped

4 cloves garlic, minced

1 red bell pepper, chopped

TO MAKE THE ORANGE SAFFRON AIOLI SAUCE

1. Finely grate zest from half of the orange. Juice the orange.

2. Put 1½ tablespoons orange juice in a small bowl with the saffron and let it stand for 10 minutes.

3. In a food processor, combine the saffron mix, orange zest, garlic, and mustard. Pulse for 15 to 20 seconds until the garlic is pureed.

4. Add the egg yolk and process for 10 seconds.

5. While the machine is still running, slowly add the oils through the feed tube. Keep processing until the sauce is thick and thoroughly incorporated.

6. Add a pinch of salt and finish blending.

7. Refrigerate the sauce 2 hours to chill.

8. When you're ready to serve, remove the sauce from the refrigerator and fold in the olives.

TO MAKE THE MUSSELS

1. Preheat the grill to medium-high.

2. Lay out four double-layered sheets of aluminum foil. Fold the edges upward into a bowl.

3. Under running cold water scrub the mussels and remove the beards.

4. Divide the mussels evenly among the four foil packs. Set them aside.

5. In a small bowl, whisk the butter, wine, lime juice and zest, olive oil, the 4 seasonings, parsley, and garlic.

6. Evenly divide the bell pepper up among the foil packs.

7. Ladle the butter mix evenly into the foil packs. Tightly seal up the packs.

8. Lightly oil the grate on the grill.

9. Place the foil packs on the grill and cook for 8 to 10 minutes, or until the shells open.

10. Transfer the mussels and any liquid to a serving bowl, and discard any mussels that didn't open. (They aren't safe, if you know what I mean...)

11. Serve with the aioli sauce.

Halibut is a mild fish, and therefore that "fishy" smell and taste isn't an issue when cooking at home. Grilling the halibut with a cedar plank deepens the flavor profile. And the use of hard wood will hopefully inspire you to have a playdate between your *other* hard wooden plank and your partner's hali-butt.

GRILL: CHARCOAL | PREP TIME: 15 MINUTES | REST TIME: 2 HOURS |
CHILL TIME: 20 MINUTES | COOK TIME: 30 MINUTES | MAKES: 4 SERVINGS

HALIBUT

1 untreated cedar plank

4 halibut steaks

½ cup butter, melted

1 tablespoon lemon juice

2 teaspoons dried tarragon

4 cloves garlic, minced

pinch of ground black pepper

4 tablespoons honey

1 tablespoon olive oil

SALSA

2 large tomatoes, finely chopped

1 large avocado, finely chopped

2 tablespoons snipped fresh chives

zest and juice of 1 lime

½ red onion, finely chopped

3 cloves garlic, minced

½ jalapeño pepper, finely minced (optional)

INSTRUCTIONS

1. Soak the hard cedar plank in water for 2 hours, keeping it submerged. You may use a full can to weigh the plank down.

2. Wash the fish and pat it dry with paper towels.

3. Let the fish rest on the paper towels while you prepare the marinade.

4. In a large bowl, combine the melted butter, lemon juice, tarragon, garlic, black pepper, and honey.

5. Set the fish in the bowl with the marinade. Ladle the marinade over the fish to really spread those juices all over, then refrigerate it for 20 minutes to let it rest. Retain the marinade for later.

6. Preheat the grill to high.

7. Place the cedar plank on the grill and cover the grill, leaving the plank alone until it starts to smoke.

8. Brush the cedar plank with the olive oil and place the fish on the plank. Cook for 20 minutes.

9. Keep a full spray bottle of water handy, in case of any flame-ups.

10. While the fish is cooking, combine the ingredients for the salsa in a bowl, then refrigerate it until you're ready to serve.

11. At this point, brush some of the marinade over the fish.

12. After 5 minutes, brush the fish again with more marinade.

13. When the fish reaches an internal temperature of 145°F, remove it from the grill.

14. Serve the halibut with the salsa.

There's no hiding lobster's message. It's a decadent dinner that will impress the dress (or pants) off any guest. Forget the restaurant reservation when you're having a crustacean craving. Rather, learn to make lobster on your own, and you've got a secret weapon when it comes to getting your own tail at home. Remember, lobster requires a bit of handiwork for preparing the thick, tender tail. This means your dinner guest will know you're real good with your hands. Don't disappoint them.

GRILL: ANY GRILL | PREP TIME: 15 MINUTES | COOK TIME: 10 TO 12 MINUTES | MAKES: 4 SERVINGS

¼ cup unsalted butter, melted

zest and juice of 2 lemons

2 tablespoons freshly chopped chives, plus more for garnish

2 tablespoons freshly chopped parsley, plus more for garnish (optional)

pinch of salt

pinch of ground black pepper

1 or 2 cloves garlic, minced

pinch of crushed red pepper

4 lobster tails

lemon wedges for serving

INSTRUCTIONS

1. Preheat the grill to high, with indirect heat on one side of the grate.

2. In a small bowl, whisk all the ingredients except the lobster tails and garnishes.

3. Using kitchen shears, cut the top of the lobster shell from the meaty portion of the tail.

4. With a knife, cut hallway through the meat, down the center, cutting all the way through the meat.

5. Insert a wooden skewer lengthwise through the meat. This prevents the meat from curling while on the grill.

6. Brush the indirect heat half the grate with olive oil.

7. Brush the butter mixture over the meaty portion of each tail and place the meat side down on the indirect heat half of the grill.

8. Cook for 5 minutes.

9. Flip the lobster tails over, brush the remainder of the butter mixture over the tails, and cook for another 5 to 7 minutes, or until the meat turns opaque and the shells turns red.

10. Remove them from the heat and plate them with garnishes.

11. Serve immediately.

NOTE: Lobster meat becomes rather unsavory when left over, so prepare only what you will eat at the initial sitting.

GRILL CHART

This chart will help you properly set the heat level on your specific grill. If your grill doesn't have a thermometer, the hands-over-grill test is the easiest way for an adult to test the grill's heat level. How you do it? Simply hold your hand over the fire until you can't anymore. Keep track of the seconds. Temperature known!

GRILL TEMPERATURE

HEAT LEVEL	TEMPERATURE	HAND-OVER-GRILL METHOD
Very Hot	600+ °F	You can't hold your hand over the fire, period.
High/Hot	400–550 °F	You can't hold your hand over the heat for more than 2 to 3 seconds.
Medium-High	350–400 °F	You can't hold your hand over the heat for more than 4 to 5 seconds.
Medium	350–400 °F	You can't hold your over the heat for longer than 6 to 7 seconds.
Medium-Low	325–350 °F	You can't hold your hand over the heat for more than 8 to 10 seconds.
Low	250–325 °F	You can hold your hand over the heat for 10 to 15 seconds.
Very Low	200–250 °F	You can feel heat but it's not really bothering your hand.

CONVERSIONS

VOLUME

US	US EQUIVALENT	METRIC
1 tablespoon (3 teaspoons)	½ fluid ounce	15 milliliters
¼ cup	2 fluid ounces	60 milliliters
⅓ cup	3 fluid ounces	90 milliliters
½ cup	4 fluid ounces	120 milliliters
⅔ cup	5 fluid ounces	150 milliliters
¾ cup	6 fluid ounces	180 milliliters
1 cup	8 fluid ounces	240 milliliters
2 cups	16 fluid ounces	480 milliliters

WEIGHT

US	METRIC
½ ounce	15 grams
1 ounce	30 grams
2 ounces	60 grams
¼ pound	115 grams
⅓ pound	150 grams
½ pound	225 grams
¾ pound	350 grams
1 pound	450 grams

TEMPERATURE

FAHRENHEIT (°F)	CELSIUS (°C)	FAHRENHEIT (°F)	CELSIUS (°C)
70°F	20°C	220°F	105°C
100°F	40°C	240°F	115°C
120°F	50°C	260°F	125°C
130°F	55°C	280°F	140°C
140°F	60°C	300°F	150°C
130°F	65°C	325°F	165°C
160°F	70°C	350°F	175°C
170°F	75°C	375°F	190°C
180°F	80°C	400°F	200°C
190°F	90°C	425°F	220°C
200°F	95°C	450°F	230°C

ABOUT THE AUTHOR

Harry Cox has spent years mastering the art of rubbing, pounding, and jerking meat. In this book, he offers his signature low-and-slow techniques for keeping your meat juicy and moist all day (and night).